FLIP IT

Prentice Hall LIFE

If life is what you make it, then making it better starts here.

What we learn today can change our lives tomorrow. It can change our goals or change our minds; open up new opportunities or simply inspire us to make a difference. That's why we have created a new breed of books that do more to help you make more of *your* life.

Whether you want more confidence or less stress, a new skill or a different perspective, we've designed *Prentice Hall Life* books to help you to make a change for the better. Together with our authors we share a commitment to bringing you the brightest ideas and best ways to manage your life, work and wealth.

In these pages we hope you'll find the ideas you need for the life *you* want. Go on, help yourself.

It's what you make it

* * *

HOW TO GET THE BEST
OUT OF EVERYTHING

FLIP IT

MICHAEL HEPPELL

Prentice Hall Life
is an imprint of

Harlow, England • London • New York • Boston • San Francisco • Toronto • Sydney • Singapore • Hong Kong
Tokyo • Seoul • Taipei • New Delhi • Cape Town • Madrid • Mexico City • Amsterdam • Munich • Paris • Milan

PEARSON EDUCATION LIMITED

Edinburgh Gate
Harlow CM20 2JE
Tel: +44 (0)1279 623623
Fax: +44 (0)1279 431059
Website: www.pearsoned.co.uk

First published in Great Britain in 2009

The right of Michael Heppell to be identified as Author of this Work has been asserted by him in accordance with the Copyright, Designs and Patents Act 1988.

ISBN: 978-0-273-72751-4

British Library Cataloguing-in-Publication Data
A catalogue record for this book is available from the British Library

Library of Congress Cataloging-in-Publication Data
A catalog record for this book is available from the Library of Congress

10 9 8 7 6 5 4 3
13 12 11 10

Typeset in Photina MT 10/14pt by 3
Printed and bound in Great Britain by Ashford Colour Press Ltd., Gosport

The publisher's policy is to use paper manufactured from sustainable forests.

For Bill Heppell

The original Flip It thinker

Contents

Introduction

I've spent the last 15 years of my life studying what we can all do to get the very best out of everything. With *Flip It* I've captured the essence of all that learning and distilled that experience into this simple but deceptively powerful book.

And it's probably going to be the easiest book you've ever read. Every idea, technique and method can be applied by anyone, from any background, in any situation, at any time, as you'll see by the many inspirational stories of people who have done just that.

Flip It offers a different, better way to think and act which, when used in the right way, will give you higher levels of happiness, confidence, creativity and success. In other words, with *Flip It* you can make everything better. Here are a couple of bold claims:

You'll become a **better person** just by **reading this book**.

You'll become an **absolutely amazing person** by putting your favourite ideas from *Flip It* into practice.

Think transferable

Flip It is broken down into several sections, each one loosely themed around an area of life – work, health, family, success, creativity, etc. But don't be fooled into thinking that some chapters will be more appropriate for you than others. Your first lesson in *Flip It* starts right now with 'Think transferrable'. It's often tempting when you see a chapter heading to make an instant judgement about the content and whether it will be applicable to you. I wonder what amazing opportunities may have passed you by thinking like that in the past?

Time for a change.

As you read each and every chapter you may find yourself thinking, 'I don't do this' or 'I don't have that in my life.' If you do, then Flip It, think transferrable and ask, 'How could I adapt and apply this technique in my life right now?' By doing this simple Flip you'll find a gem on every page.

Feel free to dive around *Flip It* and read it in any order you like. Very quickly you'll learn how to get the best out of each section. The next step is to move from knowing it to doing it. Understanding Flip It at an intellectual level is great but the real benefit comes from using the techniques in real-life situations.

The secret isn't in the
knowing it's in the **doing**.

So take action now and, as you learn a Flip It tool, test it straight away. You'll be amazed at the results and very soon you'll be the one who is getting the best out of everything.

Flip Bit
You only regret the things you didn't do – so do it.

1

Finding Flip It

So let's begin. Flip It thinking is everywhere. At times you do it without really thinking about it. There are other times when you don't do it but probably should. When you look at the cover of this book you see this symbol.

What does this mean to you?

Some people just see the cloud and immediately think it's going to be terribly dull and there's a chance of rain. Others think it will be cloudy and we may get some sun. Then there are those who bank on the fact that there will be sun interspersed with white fluffy clouds. And finally there are the super positive who just see the sun and blank out the cloud altogether.

Which are you?

With *Flip It* I want to challenge your thinking on what you see, believe and think with an ultimate goal – to help you get the best out of everything.

Let's start you off with a simple Flip and then, as you progress, we'll introduce new tools and techniques at various levels of complexity.

The power of questions

One of the most powerful tools in the Flip It toolbox is the power of intelligent questioning. The right questions can turn around any negative situation. The big question is: which questions should you ask?

Why versus How

Put on your best ringside announcer's voice as you read this:

> Ladies and gentlemen, welcome to the big fight. In the red corner, weighing in at an incredible 200 lbs, the most pondered word in anyone's vocabulary of questions. Let's hear it for: the prince of pity, the mother of misfortune, the saint of sadness, the undisputed champion of negative questioning – 'WHY'.

And in the blue corner, weighing in at a lean, mean 140 lbs, the hero of hope, the champion of chatter, the secret of solution. He's quick, he's quirky and a little bit flirty, let's hear it for the contender – 'HOW'.

Now wouldn't that be a brawl worth watching?

The word *why* is often associated with the negative. Why me? Why now? Why should I? Whereas *how* is commonly associated with solution. How can I? How do I? How should we?

Here's a classic example of *why* versus how

You're busy. You have only a few minutes to get to an important meeting and, can you believe it you're lost. In a blind panic you end up with a whole bunch of *why* questions in your head. Why do I always get lost? Why does this always happen to me? Why today of all days? The more you ask *why?*, the more your brilliant brain, with its infinite ability to keep on churning out the answers, will think of at least a dozen reasons why.

Now, let's Flip It and ask *how?* How did I end up here? How can I quickly get to where I need to be now? How can I best communicate my current situation to the people I'm due to meet? How can I stay calm?

Notice this isn't some weak but positive 'la la', isn't everything wonderful, thinking. You know, 'Hooray I'm lost, perhaps the earth's energy made this happen and I should embrace the situation.' Oh no. This is a powerful way of thinking when you need to make speedy, rational decisions, then act on them.

Why do I worry so much? How many of us anxiously brood over this classic? As it happens, asking *why* too much is often a major contributor to worry. It rarely helps you worry less. Why can't I? Why do people do that? Why is it always me?

So Flip It and ask *how*?

How can I? How can I change the way people think? How can I stop that happening again to me?

Isn't it amazing that just reading the *how* questions can make you feel better? Welcome to the world of Flip It.

Flip Bit

You can make *how* work even better if you use a bit of facial physiology too. When you ask a how question make sure you look up, if possible add a smile and raise your eyebrows. The *how* becomes more intense and your brain gets to work on a solution faster.

Isn't your brain wonderful? It contains 100 billion neurons and is capable of dealing with trillions of thoughts. Yet most of it is sitting around twiddling its thumbs waiting for something to do. So why not get your brain busy and give it some graft?

By asking yourself questions rather than taking situations as a given, you give the old brain box a bit of a blast. Here are a few examples of given situations and how you may want to turn them into questions to get better results.

I haven't got the time	Flip It	How can I find some time?
This is boring	Flip It	What can I do to make this more interesting?
I don't know	Flip It	Who do I know who knows?

By using your brilliant brain in this way, not only will you get better results for what you are thinking about right now, but you will also exercise some dormant areas of your brain. This gives you a great chance to blow out the neural cobwebs so you'll be able to use those areas effortlessly in the future.

The power of positive language

I am often labelled a 'positive thinker'. There's nothing wrong with that; but positive thinking is often nice but ineffective. I like to Flip It and incorporate positive action.

Here's a quick question for your newly awakened curious brain: what is the most common action you take?

I believe it is your *choice* of words. Whether it's your external talk (what you say to others) or your self-talk (what you say to yourself) you are constantly choosing, then using, words to communicate.

I presented at an event, and was followed on stage by Lord Melvyn Bragg. As part of my presentation I suggested there were 600,000 words in the English language. Afterwards Lord Bragg complimented me on my presentation, but remarked I might be mistaken as to the number of words in the English language. He thought there were 1.25 million!

Flip Bit

The average person has a vocabulary of around 6,000 words, so that leaves 1.19 million new words (and meanings) to choose from. Just testing out two or three new words a day would take over a thousand years.

So how about using some **Flip It** thinking on your language?

Negative to Positive

This is an area where I love to use Flip It. The idea is so simple: you just change words and phrases from negative to positive. It uses creativity, wit and wisdom plus, as a bonus, it will do wonders for your Scrabble scores.

Here are a few to get you started.

I'm tired	Flip It	I could do with a little more oomph
It's cold	Flip It	I wish it was warmer
He takes ages	Flip It	He could be quicker
I'm fat	Flip It	I could be thinner

With over one million words (and meanings) in the English language, how could you Flip It and choose to use new or better words?

Time for a time out

So you're a few pages in, and I'm guessing you'll fall into one of four camps. It's worth taking a minute to check where you are and see if you need to Flip your thinking to get the most out of this book.

Group 1: I know it

Nothing new so far? Brilliant! Whenever someone tells me they know it my response is always, 'But do you do it?' The secret isn't in the knowing, it's in the doing.

Fear not Group One, there are plenty of ideas and thinking (new ones too) that will Flip your thinking forever.

Group 2: Is it really that simple?

A question to provoke a yes and no answer. In theory yes, it is simple but you have to test it out to see what works best for you. And if some bits don't work for you that's actually good news, as you'll see later on.

Group 3: More more more!

You've already had your eyes opened and your ears are pinned back. Excellent! My advice to you is to push yourself a little further with every new chapter.

Group 4: Huh?

Don't fit in to any of the above? Perfect! You're a natural Flip It thinker. Keep going as I have a surprise for you very shortly.

What happens when you eliminate excuses?

Flip Bit

Excuses slow you down, create obstructions to creativity and barriers to trust.

When you were very small and your clever little brain was working stuff out, you realised that, if you made an excuse for not doing something, you would probably get away with it. The trouble is that was when you were five. Now you're grown up, but, you still use excuses to justify why you haven't, can't, won't, or a myriad of other negative put off's, to ensure you don't need to see something through.

If excuses are so destructive why do we use them? To discover the answer to that one you need to go back a couple of steps.

Let's bite the bullet and face a fact: an excuse is often a straight up lie. 'I couldn't do that today, I had far too much on.'

Which roughly translates as, 'Oh crikey! I've sat half the day doing nothing when I should have been doing the important stuff. Quick, think of an excuse but make it a worthy one. I know, I'll say I've been busy, no, better than that, I'll imply I've been really busy and maybe get a bit of sympathy thrown in too.'

Maybe you didn't even know you were thinking it. That's because it's hard-wired into your subconscious, so you can spout forth that kind of nonsense in a nanosecond. Well done!

So if it is 'hard-wired' can it be changed? Of course, but you'll have to Flip It first. This is going to be your first big challenge. The next time you find yourself making an excuse, Flip It and make sure your explanation is the truth. That's the truth, the whole truth and nothing but the truth.

Here are a couple of ways this may work.

A man goes to the shop. His wife asked him to pick something up while he was there and he completely forgot. When challenged he probably said something like, 'I looked all over the shop and they didn't have any, they must have sold out.'

How about you Flip It and say, 'Oh no, I completely forgot. I've no explanation but I will go straight back out and get it.'

Here's another one. 'What? You didn't get my email? We've been having a few technical problems with the system and your email must have been caught up in it.'

What if you Flip It and say, 'I'm terribly sorry I haven't sent it yet. Could you give me another hour to complete it please?'

Better? I don't know about you but, compared to poor excuses, I love a bit of honesty.

A couple of caveats.

- Don't lose your job, partner, friend or family member over this. Err on the side of caution.
- Do test yourself and push a little bit further than you would normally go.

Why bother?

There's something quite liberating about getting rid of excuses. The need to justify your actions (or lack of them) is significantly reduced. People see a new side to you, and you'll find they react to you in a different, more positive way.

Here's the best bit.

When you **eliminate excuses** you begin

to **eliminate the reasons** why you **make the excuses** in the first place.

Think about that one for a moment.

I once worked for a funny (unusual not humorous) boss who I found myself making excuses to and for. And because I didn't want to upset her I couldn't say anything. I used to get myself into a real pickle with this. Then, one day, when I was umming and erring, she looked me in the eye and said, 'The truth is freeing'.

Those words resonated in my head for a few moments then I took a deep breath and told her the truth. No one had ever told her about the problems she created and how they affected people. It was a little ugly at first, but when the air had settled, she thanked me.

I've included a whole bunch of ideas to help with this kind of situation in Chapter 8 *Flip It at work and in business.*

> **Flip Bit**
> The truth is freeing.

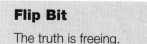

Now, let's move away from making excuses and I'll share with you one of the most magnificent uses of Flip It thinking I have ever discovered.

How to be interesting – Flip It style

Hands up if you like the idea of being thought of as an interesting person. Well that's just about everyone then. Traditional thinking dictates that, if you want to be considered interesting, you first need to be well read, bright, articulate, charming, and witty. Well, before you subscribe to that thinking read this.

A bright young psychologist took a month out from his normal work and flew back and forth every day from Los Angeles to New York (perhaps he hadn't heard of deep vein thrombosis). He would always sit in the middle seat of three.

After take off he would start a conversation with the person either side but, rather than trying to be interesting, he would Flip It and focus instead on being *interested*. All he did was ask great questions and let the other person speak.

At the end of the journey he would ask for their details on the premise he could do something for them or that they would stay in touch. One week later a researcher would call the people he had sat next to. They all remembered him. They all said how much they liked him; although none could recall if he was married, what he did for a living or where he was from (because he never told them). However, the most amazing part of the research was the fact that *over 70 per cent described him as one of the most interesting people they had EVER met!*

Flip Bit

Being interested is better than being interesting if you want be thought of as an interesting person.

Time to get a balance

This doesn't mean you won't ever have the opportunity to recount your hilarious anecdote about how Aunty Muriel almost blew up her village and how you single-handedly saved the day, but it does mean that when you Flip It you can become a master questioner and an interesting person too.

The brilliant questions Flip It

Here are 10 brilliant *being interested* questions and statements to keep in mind for the next time you meet someone.

1 How did you do that?
2 Why did you choose that?
3 Where did you learn how to do that?
4 How could someone like me get involved?
5 Can you give me an example?
6 Tell me more.
7 Would you do it again and if so what would you do differently?
8 What's next for you?
9 Really? Wow!
10 This one isn't actually anything you say. Just shut up, smile and nod. You'll be amazed at how people just keep going when you give them this cue.

Paradigm shifts

Much of what you have read so far focuses on simple Flip It thinking and actions. So it's probably about time we took it up a notch with the introduction of paradigm shifts. A paradigm shift can be described as a change in basic assumptions. We've all experienced a paradigm shift at one time or another. My challenge to you is to consciously create paradigm shifts by using Flip It thinking.

Here's an example of a time when I experienced a profound paradigm shift and what it meant to me.

I was in Washington DC attending a conference in 1995. I didn't know anyone in town and, because of my travel plans, I had arrived a day early. That night I went for a walk close to my hotel and ended up outside a cinema. Feeling a little spontaneous I asked for a ticket for whichever film was due to start next. The attendant said if I was quick a movie called *Clockers* was about to start.

I walked into the dark Screen 2, took a seat and watched the movie. As the final credits rolled and the house lights came up I looked around the room and something struck me. I was the only white person in there. I didn't feel nervous, frightened or in any way intimidated but I did feel very aware, for the first time in my life, what it was really like to be a minority.

That paradigm shift made me realise how some people must feel because of their colour, ability, size, age, etc. My wife was the only black child in a school of 700 which is unheard of nowadays but it must have had an impact on her life. Walking into that cinema taught me a wonderful lesson which I've recalled many times.

Now what if I hadn't waited for the paradigm shift to happen to me but instead took the initiative and forced the paradigm shift to happen? Here are a few paradigm shifts that you could test.

- Try spending some time in a wheelchair to see how differently people behave around you.
- Ask how a situation can be improved rather than complaining about what's wrong.
- Be your own customer.
- Fast for a day.
- Volunteer to work at a homeless shelter and talk to those attending about how they ended up there.
- Don't buy anything from a supermarket for a week and use the spare resources you have in your cupboards, freezer, etc.
- Before you condemn a person's behaviour get all the facts.

Because we can become all too familiar with our surroundings, friends, family and ways of doing things, creating and forcing a paradigm shift is often a good way to experience a different view and, in some cases, to create a powerful reality check.

Flip Bit

If you're a police traffic officer it must be weird to work your shift with everyone driving around you just within the speed limit. Then the moment you clock off and jump into your own car you experience a local version of Le Mans on your way home!

Being able to experience situations from multiple viewpoints can ensure you understand people and their behaviours better. By doing this on a consistent and regular basis you can chose to get the best out of every situation, understand things more clearly and be more equipped to deal with whatever life might throw your way.

Found Flip It?

So that's your Flip It apprenticeship over. You've got some basic thinking and some general Flip It skills. The next stage of your journey is to get specific and really master the techniques. The following chapters take many of the key areas of life and show you how to apply Flip It thinking and actions in each.

Remember to *think transferable* as you read each section. If you should catch yourself thinking, 'I'm not sure how this applies to me', then Flip It and ask, 'How can this apply to me?'

2

Flip It for confidence and happiness

Take two people; they are the same age from similar backgrounds with the exact same experience and qualifications. In fact the only difference is one has loads of confidence and the other lacks self-belief. Who's going to be the most successful?

I agree.

Over the past 10 years I've presented to over half a million people around the world. During presentations I often ask the question, 'Is there anyone here who can honestly tell me they have all the confidence they need in every area of their lives right now?' In 10 years out of 500,000 people I've only had 3 people who've put their hands up.*

Turning worry into confidence

Flip Bit

Be careful. You master what you worry about.

Unfortunately this doesn't mean you get better at it – it means you master the worrying part. Worriers have an uncanny ability to imagine the unimaginable. My mum is brilliant at it. If I call her and I'm travelling she worries about the fact I'm away from home. If I call her from home she'll worry that we can't have much work on!

People worry for many reasons but have you noticed that they are always negative things? People don't worry that they may win a contract, or find true love. No they worry that they may lose the contract or grow old lonely.

Some people claim a bit of worry is good for them. It helps them to prepare. OK, but prepare for what? The worst?

Worry is simply a product of your imagination. This is brilliant news because the better you are at using your imagination to worry, the better your imagination can be used to eliminate worry from your life. Here's how.

* I don't think they raised their hands because they did have all the confidence they needed in every area of their lives, it was that they didn't fully understand the question!

Confidence cake – the recipe for self-belief

I'm going to teach you a simple technique which is like the recipe to a perfect cake: get the ingredients right, follow the method and you'll get great results every time.

What we are going to do is use Flip It to turn worry into confidence by cleverly using the same mental muscle that creates the worry in the first place – your amazing imagination.

Test out this idea right now. Then practise some more. And then a little more. Then, the next time you feel worry coming your way, you will be able to use it immediately.

Think of a time in your past when you were worried about something and you actually needn't have worried at all as the situation turned out really well and you ended up feeling incredibly confident.

Here are a couple you may have experienced to get your mind turning.

- A date that turned from stress to success.
- A new job interview that moved from concern to contract.
- A theatre performance that transformed from stage fright to leading light.

Now cast your mind back to the time just before the worry started to set in, and run through the order of events until you get to the point where you ultimately felt incredibly confident.

Now evaluate the differences between the worried you and the confident you. Make a note of the variation in:

- breathing;
- physiology;
- focus;
- language;
- image colour and size;
- reaction of people around you.

You may find it easier to do the next bit with your eyes closed.

Take the feelings and actions of confidence you have just experienced and make them bigger and bolder in your imagination. Now supercharge them until you can feel yourself glowing with confidence!

Now practise this confidence recipe as often as you can. And give this way of feeling a name: Super Me, Confidence Man, Wonder Woman, you get the idea. This can feel a little false and weird at first. That's OK, so did riding a bike and tying your shoe laces, but you don't even think about that now. And, in just the same way, the more you practise the confidence recipe the more powerful it will become until it is like second nature to you.

So, the next time you feel yourself starting to worry, immediately Flip It and start to use your new confidence recipe. Hold this for as long as you can, which may be several minutes or even hours. You have to really go for it, believe it will work and stick with it.

Flip Bit

For people who can turn worry into confidence the rewards are extraordinary.

Using cloudy nostalgia

Nostalgia isn't what it used to be (sorry I couldn't resist). But, on a serious note, have you noticed how two eye witness reports of the same event can appear completely different? And how often people change their memory of events to the outcome they would like? This is because memory is just your interpretation of what really happened.

This is one of those strange phenomena that can be manipulated to your advantage by using Flip It (and a bit of imagination) to take unhelpful memories and recreate them into a positive past.

I use the word 'unhelpful' carefully here as it may be that some negative parts of your past may need to remain. I'll let you be the judge of that.

Daniel was a reasonably happy 40-year-old, but he found it difficult to connect with his father. As his father was getting on a bit, Daniel wanted to fix this and decided to use 'cloudy nostalgia' to do it. It turns out that

Daniel's father wasn't around for him much when he was a child. At least that was how he remembered it.

Daniel thought it was time to create a better memory. He started by visiting his mum and asking her to recount some of her favourite memories of him as a child with his dad. Much to his surprise, she had lots. Fun fights, fishing trips, the day he got locked in a loo and dad had to climb over the door and many more.

Then Daniel did the same exercise with his dad.

Next, Daniel took 15 minutes to visit his memory, with a healthy dose of imagination packed in his pocket. He went back as far as he could remember and played out moments where he and his dad had had great times together. He then started to weave in some extra times along with those that had been shared by his mum and dad. Every time he came to a point that he had associated with his father not being around, he created a new memory and played it over and over in his imagination.

The more he did this, the more his memory and imagination merged and the more happy childhood memories of time he spent with his dad were created.

'At first I felt like a fake,' says Daniel, recalling how his new memories were created, 'but after a short while I found it easier to mix and merge memory with imagination. The weird thing was how much more positive I felt towards my dad. He hadn't changed – or had any need to – but I had.'

Flip Bit

It's never too late to have a happy childhood.

Act 'as if'

You may think that using imagination and memory like this is a little far fetched. I know I needed to be convinced when I first started to explore methods for increasing confidence and self-belief.

Simon Woodroffe, one of Britain's most successful entrepreneurs, who founded YO! Sushi and YOtel, once told me that even he worries that one day he'll be 'found out'. When I asked how he overcame this, he said he 'acted as if'.

When he was negotiating the deal for his first YO! Sushi restaurant he didn't really have a clue what he should be saying or doing so he simply acted 'as if' he did know. Simon says, 'I would get into the mindset of a person who was an expert and I'd ask myself, "How would they do this?" then I'd act that part as best I could.'

When you **don't know how** to handle something, Flip It and **act 'as if'** you do. It's **amazing** what will pop into your mind.

Here's a secret for you. Most of us have huge self-doubt so we look for people who have certainty so we can believe in them. Could that be you?

Flip Bit

The first person to convince is you. If you can convince yourself you can convince anyone.

How would a confident person act? What would you do if you were certain? What would be different if you eliminated doubt? One way to do this is to create different characters (using the confidence recipe) who can be at your fingertips when you need them. So as well as Super Me you might also have Meeting Maestro or Hot Date Girl.

Your act 'as if' characters can have multiple personalities too.

Confident	Compassionate	Innovative	Considerate
Certain	Inspired	Funny	Shrewd
Clever	Determined	Cool	Relaxed

Practising acting 'as if' when you don't need to is vital; practise does after all make perfect, so when you do need to pull off an Oscar-winning performance you'll be ready.

Next ball

Richard Nugent is the co-author with Steve Brown of *Football: Raise your mental game* (A. & C. Black, 2008). He coaches top footballers and sportspeople, as well as company leaders. We were discussing why some footballers just seem to lose their confidence during a match and he told me an amazing story about one of his clients.

His client was a Liverpool player who could be described as being one of the brightest young players in the country. But he had a dilemma. If he made a poor pass early in the game he could guarantee that he would make at least another five poor passes in the rest of the match.

The mental challenge was he would hold on to the memory of his last poor pass. This meant that not only was he playing each new pass but he was also replaying the poor one he had made previously.

Richard explained, 'That means you are now trying to make two good passes at the same time and because the brain doesn't differentiate well between what's real and what's strongly imagined, no matter how good at football you are, playing two passes at the same time is difficult!'

You can imagine how this would create anxiety. Each time he would make another poor pass it would build on the mental challenge, becoming three, four and so on and replaying over and over.

This young footballer would build up a layer of poor passes and with each one would become more and more certain that he would play another poor pass. And with that certainty his passes indeed became poorer.

To fix the problem, Richard taught his client to focus on using a trigger phrase, which was 'next ball'. He would repeat this phrase over and over to himself while playing, and in doing so eliminate the memory of a poor pass.

So if you're a professional footballer reading this you know what to do if you're making poor passes. But the chances are you're not. Your equivalent of a poor pass could be: rejection, a missed opportunity, a failed audition, the way someone reacts to you, messing up what you were going to say.

If you create a phase such as 'next ball' for whatever it is that affects you it makes it less likely you'll make a mistake again. By focusing on the positive 'next' rather than reliving a negative 'past' you build your confidence quickly.

The 'next ball' Flip It

Here are some examples to get you started.

- A poor telephone conversation – 'next call'.
- Not sure what to say when meeting someone – 'next words'.
- Forgetting your words when presenting – 'next line'.
- Not getting something done – 'next action'.
- Your suggestion gets rejected – 'next idea'.

Still ordering number 37?

But what if you associate your past with safety? Then it becomes difficult to experience new things because your perception of anything new or different is associated with risk.

When I was a child it was a big treat to order a Chinese takeaway. I remember the ceremony. About once a month my Mum or Dad would announce that we were having Chinese. My brother and I would get quite excited and 30 minutes later Dad would arrive home with a plastic carrier bag containing: 1 Chicken Fried Rice (number 37), 1 Sweet and Sour Chicken (number 52) and a portion of chips.

I genuinely believed for the first 13 years of my life that the only food you could get from our local Chinese takeaway was Chicken Fried Rice, Sweet and Sour Chicken and a portion of chips!

My parents had ordered the same Chinese meal for 20 years. Why? It was safe, it tasted nice and they knew what they were getting.

Here's how and why they changed their minds and in doing so helped me discover the wonders of international cuisine.

After telephoning the order, my Dad arrived home with the bag. I recall his exact words when he took off the lid and discovered the Chicken Fried Rice had been mixed up with a House Special Chow Mein: 'Bloomin' heck Liz, what's that?' (I didn't hear my dad swear until I was 16.)

I remember them peering into the tin foil container, and then scooping out a noodle with a fork. After a few minutes of probing and discussion I said, 'Look, I'll have it.' To which my Mum replied, 'But you don't like noodles.'

How would she know? I'd never had them!

Finally, we decided that the best thing to do was to all taste a little. It turned out that everyone loved it.

But that wasn't what encouraged the Heppell family to deviate from Number 37 and 52 and try multiple Chinese dishes. The real reason was far more complicated than that.

Although I now know that this strange new food was House Special Chow Mein (number 78), at the time it was known just as 'the mistake'. On those special occasions that we had Chinese food, my dad would order our usual oriental fare but then he would attempt to describe 'the mistake' dish hoping to relive the glory of the House Special Chow Mein.

It took six attempts over several months but, in the end, he found it. Plus we found five other new dishes, which inevitably we loved.

What's your equivalent of a number 37? What do you do, because you always have?

Perhaps it's time to Flip It and test out something new. Use it as a confidence-building exercise, whether it be food, a holiday, a route, or a new way of doing something.

Flip Bit

My friend Cheryl says, 'Every three years you should change your house, your husband or your job.'

Failing a test, screwing up the interview or that awful first date

If you ever want to either have your confidence boosted or have it knocked right out of you then sit a test. If you do well your confidence will soar and if you do badly your confidence will take a dive.

So what could I suggest to help prepare you for taking exams? Oh yes EXAMS – **E**xaggerated an**X**iety **A**nd **M**ental **S**tress.

And as if taking the exam wasn't bad enough the next stage is worse – getting your results. Stop for a moment and ask yourself how can the opening of an envelope dictate how clever you are? Are you any more or less intelligent the moment after you read the result than the second before? So why do we give ourselves such a hard time when we fail a test?

Time to Flip It and get the best out of the situation.

I'm a big fan of learning; I'm not such a big fan of the current methods of testing our learning. Sometimes we are judging whether a person is good at something because they were good at taking an exam in that subject. Does this mean they are better than someone who can apply the ideas in real life more effectively but isn't as good at taking an exam?

So what can you do if you fail a test?

1 Destroy the result. If you have failed completely then get rid of the evidence. Burn it, shred it, anything, but don't hold on to it.

2 Convince yourself you are the same person you were just a few moments before. But now you have something extra – experience.

3 If you are going to re-sit do it as soon as you can. This is very important particularly with driving tests.

4 Get feedback. If there is someone who can explain why you didn't pass, ask them why you didn't – and listen.

5 Ask yourself, 'What have I learned?'

6 Use a confidence booster like the ones outlined earlier in this chapter.

Failing a test needn't be a nightmare. By flipping the experience you can turn a negative into a positive learning experience.

The same applies to getting over that disastrous first meeting with your new flame's parents or not getting the job of your dreams.

The more confidence you have, the easier it is to get out of your comfort zone. The more you get out of your comfort zone the more confidence you have. Waiting for one or the other to happen is not a strategy.

You have to Flip It and take action by working on building your confidence and your confidence will build you.

Flip Bit

Everyone wants more confidence but very few consciously work to build theirs.

The good news is you're not everyone.

Being happy for the heck of it

Most people wait for a reason to be happy then they choose to be cheerful. Flip It suggests you don't need to feel happy first for happy things to happen. In fact you can create a happy state any time you choose.

But being happy for the heck of it needs some strategies. This section is designed to get you started.

Don't overanalyse these questions, just answer a simple yes or no to the following.

Can you be happy and sad in the same day?

Can you be happy and sad in the same hour?

Have there been times in your past when a similar situation has made you feel happy one time and sad the next?

Have you noticed how some people appear to be happier than others?

Have you noticed how some people appear to be happy all the time?

Are there times when, even if you have a lot to be happy about, it's easier to be a bit grumpy or a bit sad?

In fact, can you choose to be grumpy?

Isn't grumpy a lovely word?

And now the big one ... If you can choose to be grumpy (or sad) can you also choose to be happy?

My guess is that you will have answered yes to most of the questions. These simple questions are just a way to get you thinking about the fact that you *do* have a choice. That choice becomes even more obvious when you have the right tools.

Flip Bit

You have a choice. Be grumpy or be happy.

A simple way to Flip It from sad to happy

The easiest and fastest way to start is to put a big daft grin on your face and see what happens. Yes I know this can be a lot harder to do than it is to say (and it's even easier to read) but it's still worth the effort. There are two schools of thought for this type of 'fake it until you make it' thinking.

The first goes along the lines of when you take an action, even if you don't believe it, you can trick your mind into thinking a different way and you'll get different results.

The other is that all you are doing is applying a thin film over your deeper thought processes and even if it does make a difference you quickly revert back to where you were previously.

I think a combination of the two is a little more realistic, so here's my 'sad-to-happy in three steps' guide. You'll get some quick results – and they'll last too.

- **Step 1   Change your physiology:** That means change your face from a smirk to a smile, put your shoulders back, activate your eyes, look up and take a couple of deep breaths.

- **Step 2   Explore what's right:** This means you need to find five things that are right and good about this moment. I'm alive, I live in a nice house, I look good, people like me for who I am, I get to eat today! You know the sort of thing, but you need five as a minimum and it works a little better if you write them down.

- **Step 3   Action stations:** Take one or two actions towards creating a happier state – and by action I mean move it! When you are sedentary it's easier to feel sad, when you are moving it's easier to feel happy. If you need to call a friend then stand up and move to a different room to do it. If you need to sort out a mess then move swiftly to do it.

There's some feel-good
emotion in your **motion**!

Simple? Too simple? Well don't knock it until you've tested it and it's best to test it before you need it.

Don't wait for a time when you're down, **practise now** and it will then be **easy for you** to apply when you need it.

If you're a cover to cover reader (as opposed to a dipper, like me!) you will have noticed you're about 20 per cent of the way through *Flip It* and it's time to move on from you, you, you and expand your thinking to incorporate ...

3

Flip It for friends, love and family

It would be great if this could be the shortest chapter of the book, but all too often we take our loved ones for granted and in the process create unnecessary challenges for ourselves. Like any area of life, your relationships with family and friends can be better (or much better) with some tools, techniques and a bit of effort.

Friends

Let's start with your friends. Friends are wonderful; when you want to spend time with them, they're aligned to your beliefs, not too needy, generous and supportive. You know your friends and they know you. They know exactly what to buy you for Christmas and birthdays and they never outstay their welcome. They call you at just the right time, remember what's important and they have sixth sense when it comes to giving sympathy or advice in just the right amounts at the right time. Does that sound like your friends?

Most likely your friends do a bit of all of the above now and then, scattered thinly with a healthy dose of calling when it's most inconvenient, showing off, talking about you behind your back, buying you ill thought-out gifts (that aren't nearly as good as the ones you bought them) and not really understanding you, your needs, wants and desires.

Or have I been too mean because yours land flatly somewhere in between? 'Hey they're my friends there's not much I can do!', I hear you cry.

What if you were to Flip It and make a decision that you weren't happy with second best and wanted to get the finest out of your friendships? Well now is as good a time as any to start.

The friends grid

Let's start by making a list of your top eight friends who you spend most of your time with. Write their names on the list opposite. They can be neighbours, work colleagues, old school friends, etc. Then next to each name make a rough calculation of how much of your time you spend with each one. To make this easy assume you are awake and available to spend time with other people for approximately 100 hours a week.

Now take a moment to give them a score from 1–10 on the following scales.

How positive or negative ($+$ or $-$)they are. Very positive would be a 9 or 10 and negative would be a 2 or 3. They may of course be somewhere in-between. Make 5 your neutral point.

Here are a few examples to help you to score.

Positive (high scores)	Negative (low scores)
Focuses on what's right	Talks about what's wrong
Searches for a solution	Looks at the problem
Leaves you energised	Leaves you exhausted
Loves to smile	Loves a good moan

Next score the amount they 'Give or take' in the relationship. Again measure this as very giving being high and taking being low. Again make 5 your neutral point.

Here are a few examples to help you make your score.

Giving (high scores)	Taking (low scores)
Interested in you	Always wants to talk about themselves
Knows and understands your foibles	Doesn't know the real you
Volunteers first, asks questions later	Wants to know everything
First to put their hand in their pocket	Last to the bar!

Friend	Percentage of time	+ or −	Give or take
1 _____	% _____	_____	_____
2 _____	% _____	_____	_____
3 _____	% _____	_____	_____
4 _____	% _____	_____	_____
5 _____	% _____	_____	_____
6 _____	% _____	_____	_____
7 _____	% _____	_____	_____
8 _____	% _____	_____	_____

OK, that's probably been quite tough so well done if you've completed the first eight names. Now, assuming you have done the exercise, you can plot where your friends land on this simple grid.

I've added a couple of examples so you can see how it works. In the example below, Tom received a 6 for being a giving person but only a 3 on the negative to positive scale. So he lands in the top left quadrant. Sue on the other hand is very positive and giving and ends up in the top right quadrant.

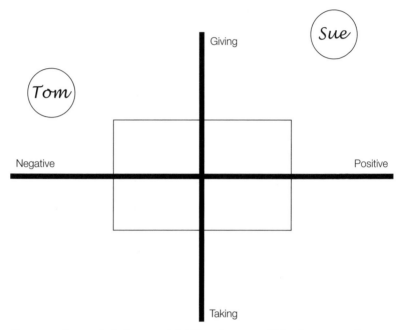

Once you have plotted your eight friends, you will begin to see who you should consider spending more time with and those for whom you may need to develop some different strategies.

Here's my description of the four quadrants.

- **Sappers**: You feel like all your energy has been drained after you spend time with them. You appreciate them as friends but understand that they are focused mainly on two things: themselves and what's wrong with life.

  We've all had times like these but if your friend is a 'sapper' and you spend a high percentage of your time with them then you need to take some action to protect yourself.

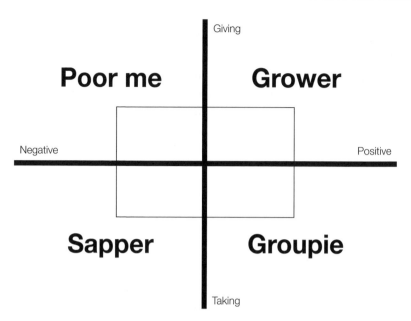

- **Poor me**: They are very nice giving people, but ... every encounter leaves you feeling sorry for them. Sometimes this makes you feel guilty that they are so giving and perhaps you're not.

  'Poor me' people also tend to suffer from illness more and, as much as they don't want you to worry, they'll be happy to share with you all the gory details.

- **Groupies**: Always chirpy and smiling and usually ready to tell you all about what they have done. They seem to have a little bit of knowledge and lots of opinions about pretty much everything. The challenge comes because they feel like they always have to be right and invariably you'll soon feel like you're forever wrong.

- **Growers**: Wow! They make you feel good. They're interested and interesting. They care and love to have fun by doing the things you want to do. When it comes to support they're there for you. You're happy to listen to their advice because you've usually asked for it.

Do those descriptions sound apt?

Now my friends are in the grid – what next?

When my wife Christine and I first created the 'friends grid', we tested it with some of our mates. It was amazing to see their reactions as they discovered why they felt differently about some pals and friendship groups. After a couple of minutes of consideration they all asked the same question: now what do we do?

Here's your choice. If you are really happy with your friends, the time you spend with them and what you get out of the relationship then you needn't do anything. But this book is about Flipping It and getting the best out of everything – and that includes your friendships.

Here are a few thoughts about what you may wish to do with the friends in each quadrant.

Let's start with what I call the '3E' line. It starts at the top right, goes through the centre and ends at the bottom left.

The closer your friends are to the top right of the grid the more you should focus on the first E and 'elevate' them.

The closer your friends are to the bottom left of the grid, the more you should consider the third E and work out how you can 'eliminate' them.

OK, time for time out. When I say eliminate I don't mean call up a few dodgy guys in heavy overcoats. And I'm not suggesting that if a friend is in need of help and finds themself there due to current circumstances that you immediately block them out of your life. But I am implying that you may have to take some action to protect yourself from the people who routinely end up here. I really do believe you can do this in a positive way.

People who land in the central area of the line can be 'upgraded' with a little of the final E – 'education'. This makes anyone who lands on this centre bottom left to top right line easy: 3E's elevate, educate or eliminate. Now here's the detail on the quadrants.

- **Sappers**: Take a look at the hours you spend with sappers and ask what you can do to halve this amount of time as quickly as you can. Remember, you become like the people you spend most of your time with.

- **Poor me**: This is a challenging one as these friends love to give but take a lot back emotionally. The best way to deal with them is through 'tough love'. It may be the case that you have to sit down with them and tell them how you feel about their negativity. Encourage them to look at the positive side of a situation.

- **Groupies**: This bunch are great in groups. Plan your time so there are others around when you meet with groupies. You'll find that it's easier to manage the amount of energy they need when it is divided between a few of you.

- **Growers**: Spend more time with these people. Especially if they are in the high top right corner. If you have managed to halve the time you spend with the sappers replace it with the growers!

> **Flip Bit**
>
> Tell your friends in the 'growers' quadrant how much you appreciate and value them. They'll love it.

Friendly rivalry

I bet you have some friends you feel you are in competition with. And I bet you have some friends who feel like they are in competition with you. And while we're being honest I bet you focus more of your energy on the people who you consider to be better than you.

I'm sure this began when we were teenagers (or even younger) when it seemed like everyone you knew had something or did something better than you.

I had a very wise uncle who, when I would nag him about how everyone seemed to have whatever it was I wanted, he would say, 'Michael, you will always feel like you're not as good as some, but you'll also know you are much better than others.'

By being in competition with friends, family and colleagues there are going to be times when you feel like you just don't measure up. These feelings don't make you any better but there are actions you can take which will make you feel great.

Time to Flip It. Spending time with people who are better than you is brilliant if you want to up your game and if these people are your friends then that's something to celebrate. Park the envy and focus on what you can learn from friends like these.

Now let's Flip It again and consider some of your friends who no doubt feel you are better than them. If that's the case then at all costs avoid arrogance. It sneaks up, and before you know where you are, wham you're bragging. Sometimes when you thought you were just sharing the exciting things that were happening to you, your friends heard it as arrogance. If you're in doubt, take some time out.

Have a snack – a nice **big slice** of **humble pie**.

Flip Bit

You can't choose your family but you can choose your friends. Choose well, choose to be brilliant with your friendships and your friends will choose to be brilliant with you.

Love

Being in love is the ultimate positive state. When you find love it magnifies everything that's amazing about life; it's like the very best friendship on fire! And as with anything so remarkable and precious, it takes luck and a bit of effort to find and a mountain of skill to sustain.

If you're in love I will share with you some methods for maintaining and boosting it. If you haven't found love, have loved and lost or don't know what all the fuss is about, we'll start with you.

Finding love – Flip It style

'One day my prince will come' is a statement that is as romantic as it is unlikely: 1 Princes rarely just show up; 2 if they do they are normally so full of themselves you won't fancy them; 3 'once upon a time in a land far, far away' isn't now and you're here!

So which do you think will work best: sit around and hope that Mr/Ms Right will stumble across you eventually? Or get out there and find them for yourself? I know it might feel frightening but, yes, it is number two.

I'm going to split the next section into two parts. The first is written by me for men. The second is written by my wife Christine for women. *I would suggest the women should not read the men's section as you may not like the advice. Similarly, lads don't read the girls' bit.*

Information for men

Here's a simple list of dos and don'ts if you are looking for love.

- Do (you'd better) shape up – Olivia Newton-John was right! Love handles don't attract love.
- Don't try to be pretty – women don't like blokes who spend longer getting ready than they do.
- Do have clean shoes, nails and teeth.
- Don't think heavily scented deodorant attracts women – no matter what the adverts say.
- Do make the first move. Women find a confident man very attractive but, be careful, women find an arrogant man repulsive.
- Don't focus on rejection. Unless you are very, very lucky you will have to face some rebuffs to find the love of your life.
- Do be romantic, but not if you have just been introduced and not in front of her friends – keep it real.
- Don't agree with everything she says just for the sake of it.
- Do be polite.
- Don't talk only about you, no matter how hilarious you are!
- Do talk about her – especially if you show genuine interest (see 'How to be interesting – Flip It style' on page 9)

Information for women

OK girls, your turn.

- Do stay in shape – not only will you look better but you'll feel better too.

- Don't smoke – it isn't sexy, it's bad for you, you'll smell – oh, and it gives you cellulite.

- Do let your friends fix you up – honestly, it won't ever be as bad as you think.

- Don't 'look for a husband' – unless you want to scare off every man within 50 miles.

- Do smile a lot – men find smiles incredibly attractive, although make sure it's a genuine smile, otherwise you might look a bit of a loon.

- Don't think men know it all – often they haven't got a clue so they need to be guided.

- Do be safe.

- Don't be too late – fashionably is 5–10 minutes, after that it's verging on rude.

So you followed my advice and didn't even dream of reading the other list. Or did you decide to Flip It and take a sneaky peak? Thought so – we are fascinated in what the other sex wants.

So are you ready to go for it? Well what are you waiting for? Oh yes, the actual 'how you meet someone' bit.

Meeting the love of your life

You probably won't meet that special someone sitting in front of your TV wishing your life away. But you may just meet them sitting in front of your PC. Did you know that one in eight people who got married in America in 2007 met online? Online dating has evolved massively over the last few years.

Here's a little secret about people who are using online dating sites to meet someone – they want to meet someone. The same can't be said in bars, clubs and parties, where you have to dance around the whole 'are you looking' routine before you can move on.

So if you don't want to move much further than your laptop to get started, could you park your prejudice and go online?

Now what about getting out there, exploring real life and meeting strangers? Arrrgggghhh. But what if I get rejected? What if I fail? What if I'm the ugliest person in the room? What if I'm the only single person there?

OK, time to Flip It. What if there are lots of single people there? What if people find you incredibly good-looking? What if you get a date? What if you find love?

I have a male friend who could walk into a room genuinely believing every woman in there would be attracted to him. He was 'no oil painting' as my grandmother would say, but he always found several women who found him appealing. And when he did face rejection he would be polite, smile, move on and quietly say to himself 'next'.

Nurturing new love

OK, you've got over the biggest hurdle and met someone. You like them, they like you, you really enjoy each other's company. Could this be … love?

I was asked in an interview to define 'being in love'. I described it like this: 'It's when your heart skips a beat as your partner walks through the door'. If you can still say that after loving your wife for 20 years and still feel your heart skip, then I think you've cracked it.

I don't think you can rely on luck to get you there.

There are three levels in a relationship. Once the honeymoon period of a new relationship has ended (and it will) then you must focus on upgrading your relationship to level 3.

- **Level 1   What can I get out of this?** It's where most relationships start, and that's fine, but if you keep thinking like this your relationship is unlikely to develop

- **Level 2   I'll do this for you, but I expect you to do that for me.** This is a quid pro quo type of thinking and the place where most relationships develop then stop. Many people are happy with this as it creates a certain degree of certainty. For example, 'You went out on Tuesday night with your friends, so it's OK if I go out with mine on Thursday.'.

- **Level 3 Your needs are my needs.** This is the ultimate place for a relationship to progress to. You are totally committed to your partner's needs and they are to yours without expectation of anything in return. And, as you might expect, getting there is tough but staying there is tougher. However, the rewards are amazing.

A level 3 relationship really needs Flip It thinking as it requires trust and commitment at the highest level. It's also essential that both people are at that level. Can you imagine a relationship with one person at level 3 and the other at level 1?

Love to listen

Here's a tip for the blokes. You know when you and the missus get in from work and she's had one hell of a day and wants to tell you all about it?

She's describing her shenanigans in glorious technicolor and midway you think you've got the answer to her problems and you can save her. So you chip in with your logical male wisdom, but she doesn't really seem to be listening to you. But you're convinced you can fix it for her.

Then the realisation. She hasn't listened to a word you've said. All that brilliant 'manvice' and it didn't make a jot of difference. Now you're frustrated, she's even more wound up and you were only trying to help!

It might look something like this:

Man: ⁶Hi sweetheart, how was your day?⁹

Woman: ⁶Fine … except …⁹

Man: ⁶Except what?⁹

Woman: ⁶My boss is driving me nuts. He completely overlooks me, gives me all the crappy jobs and nit-picks over the smallest things.⁹

Man [here comes the ⁶manvice⁹]: ⁶You know what you should do?⁹

Woman: ⁕There's nothing I can do, he's the boss.⁕

Man: ⁕Rubbish! If I were you I would …⁕

Woman: ⁕But you're not me!⁕

Man: ⁕I know, I wouldn't have let it get this far, but now that you have, here⁕s what you should do.⁕

Woman: ⁕You have no idea what I have to do or what I can and can't do.⁕

If that sounds like a familiar fail it's because it breaks the first law of male/female relationships.

Men want to fix things and **women want** to be heard.

Don't assume that because a woman is having issues, she'd ideally like a man to come along and fix them for her. Generally speaking, if a woman needs something fixed she'll fix it herself (unless it's self-assembly furniture) or she'll ask.

Similarly, if you're a woman and you're speaking to a man, don't assume he's listening (unless you're telling him the full-time scores). God was feeling quirky when configuring the male and female brains.

So let's Flip It and re-run the same situation, but this time let's use this newfound knowledge.

Man: ⁕Hi sweetheart! How was your day?'.

Woman: ⁕Fine … except …'

Man: ⁕Except what?'

Woman: ⁕My boss is driving me nuts. He completely overlooks me, gives me all the crappy jobs and nit-picks over the smallest things.'

Man: ⁕Tell me more.⁕

Woman: *Oh, you know, I probably take it too personally, but in the last week there must have been half a dozen times when he's made me feel like a second-class citizen.*

Man: *Really? Tell me more.*

Woman: *Oh, there's no more. I'm just venting.*

Man: *I know, but I'm happy to listen. Tell me about it.*

Woman: *Well, on Tuesday ...*

Got that fellas? Good.

Now here's a tip for the ladies.

When your bloke gets in from work, let him watch the news or sport in his 'cave' (the lounge) for half an hour or so before you attempt any form of sensible communication.

That's it. Simple. But then men are.

Men and women are different in many ways. *The same differences that make intimate relationships wonderful one day, can destroy them the next.* Recognising this and enhancing the good parts whilst eliminating the bad parts is the key to a successful loving relationship.

Lasting love

I've been in love with my wife for more of my life than I haven't. That's pretty good going when you're only 41.

I've found that invariably it's the little things that can make or break a relationship. Those small things that show you love, care about and respect someone are so vital. Get them right and you've got a rock-solid foundation for your love.

Here are a few of the things we do for each other – see if they inspire you to come up with your own small ways of showing how important you are to each other.

● **Getting a pasting:** Whenever we go to bed, whoever goes into the bathroom first puts the toothpaste on both toothbrushes. I can't remember when or why we started to do this, but it's both simple and lovely.

- **Vintage texting:** Leaving love notes isn't a new idea, but thanks to the advent of texting it's a lost one. Yes, it is lovely to receive a text from your partner but finding a hand-written note in your sock drawer is magical.

- **Icy start**: One of the most amazing things my wife does for me is that she defrosts my car in the winter. I can't tell you how wonderful it feels to get into a warm car with a clear windscreen, especially when you are in a hurry.

- **Mix tape**: It's never been easier to create a special CD for your lover thanks to iTunes and other music players. Just create the playlist, stick in a CD and click 'burn'. But you can make it even more special by writing an accompanying track listing with why you chose each song.

- **Saying 'I love you'**: How many times would you have to hear those words before you got sick of them? Exactly. So if you haven't said it today, tell him or her right now.

So there's a start for you. Finding love is the most amazing experience you will have. And who knows, when love goes well and relationships blossom the next step for many is to grow that love and start a family.

Family

Oh yes, good old family. Let's start with an easy one.

How to get your kids to clear their plates and tidy their rooms without asking them.

I carried out a training day for a further education college prior to their inspection. They were very busy and couldn't close the college for a day, so we had to hold the training on a Saturday.

On the posters and invitations the organisers listed what staff would learn if they were prepared to give up their day off and come to my presentation. Last on the list was one sentence which read: 'Find out how to get your kids to tidy their bedrooms without asking, bribing or nagging.'

Some 98 per cent of the college staff turned up! Guess what they all wanted to know? You got it.

The brilliance of this technique is that it can be used to encourage anyone to do almost anything. I bet that's got your attention.

Here's how it works. Children, especially teenagers, come pre-programmed with an automatic aversion to tidying their rooms. Most parents use nagging and cajoling to try and persuade their kids to tidy up. It doesn't work. So what do they do? The crazy parents push harder.

Faced with this exact predicament with our son, Christine and I halted our conventional thinking and decided to Flip It. Our idea was radical and came with a fair amount of risk.

From that day on, we decided to give only positive feedback to our son Michael about his room. We would search for somewhere he'd made tidy, put something away or cleaned and compliment him on it. Some days that was a tough call!

After initial confusion, including the revelation from him that, 'he knew exactly what we were doing' we stuck with it. It took around two weeks to see a difference but slowly and surely his room became tidier. In fact, much tidier!

Conventional **persuasion techniques** don't often persuade they just appear to

be easier and provide a **quick fix**. Families deserve more.

Building on what's right

Imagine for a moment you focused all your energy on what was right with your family. What might it be like? Most families, for one reason or another, end up being lazy in their relationships. At first it's not a big deal, but then when things are going wrong they try to fix it but it's too late.

I've met fathers who focus more on 'the business deal' than they do on their beautiful daughters. I've seen wives who care more about promotion than they do about their partner. And too many husbands who care more about their ego than they do about anyone or anything.

It's easy to be lazy in a family relationship because often the cost isn't clear until it's too late. Families forgive faster than friends. Families will take more crap than colleagues. And families make excuses for their loved ones and put up with more than is necessary.

Face it – we can all do better.

Here are 10 things you can do with relatives from your closest to your most extended that are guaranteed to make a family fantastic.

1 **Start dating** (your partner): When you first met your partner how much effort did you put in to your relationship? How much time did you spend preparing for a date? You were on time, you looked great, you created excitement and you cared – really cared. You gave compliments and focused on all the things that were right about your partner. How much of that could you revive or refresh?

2 **Record your parents** (or grandparents): I've recently started to record my parents telling stories about their past. It's amazing what you don't know or have forgotten. The best bit is with the advent of new technology it's never been easier to record and store these tales for future nostalgia.

3 **Eat together**: Most families don't and it's such a shame. The family meal is a fantastic way to catch up with each other at the end of a busy day to share and care.

4 **'Date' your children:** If you have children, find opportunities to have time with them one on one. I have fond memories of a time I took my daughter to a fancy restaurant and she could hardly see over the edge of the table.

5 **Dads' and lads' days:** Mums can have their version of these days too, but there's nothing quite like a bit of male bonding. Grrrrr.

6 **Spend longer with older relatives**: I've found myself saying, 'I haven't got much time' before I've even got through the door when visiting some of my older relatives. If you've done that too it's time to Flip It and find a way to share a little more of your day.

7 **Give great presents:** Most people don't really think about what to give family members and often end up giving a voucher or cheque. It really is a limiting belief to use language like, 'I never know what to give them.' Flip It and instead ask yourself, 'What would be a brilliant present for …'?

8 **Have a gathering:** Make contact with your extended family and have a reunion. Go on I dare you. This could be the only time your family come together when it's not a wedding or funeral.

9 **Gather some souvenirs for your siblings:** You knew your brothers and sisters when they were kids ('cos you were too). These unique relationships give you an exceptional opportunity to put together a memory box, scrap book or album that only the two of you will truly understand.

10 **Tell them how much you love them:** Saying 'I love you' to a family member can be a stretch if you're not used to it but as I said before who do you know who doesn't want to hear it? Share the love – verbally.

Working on relationships is challenging but very rewarding, especially when you are faced with one of life's tragic but great certainties.

The loss of a loved one

It is an inevitable part of life that people will die. Can Flip It help during these times? I believe so. In fact I believe that often our own Flip It thinking takes over naturally during these times. We remember what we cherished about the person, we come together, we show compassion and we care.

During the process of grieving many people feel guilt. They may be aware that they haven't seen or spoken to a person for some time. Perhaps some things were left unsaid or they could have given more to the relationship.

Grieving is a natural and expected process. Some people appear to be dealing with the loss of a loved one very well by refusing to grieve, only for their grief to manifest in other ways. There are three stages of grief.

- **Stage 1 Shock:** Often people feel shocked and have a sense of disbelief when they experience the loss of a loved one. This can last from a few hours to days or weeks. At this time the distress comes in waves, which are often triggered by emotional stimuli.

    If you lose someone close it can be very difficult to find time for yourself to actually mourn. There are arrangements to make, visitors to care for and all this without a person who would usually be there to support you. Here's a time when you can Flip It and ask to be left alone to grieve.

- **Stage 2 Confrontation:** The feeling of loss at this stage is high and the ability to cope seems distant. People deal with this in many ways. They have difficulty sleeping and eating, search for reasons for the loss, feel distant, withdraw socially, feel guilty and can express anger for what other people have in their lives. At this time of wanting to be shut off from the world it's actually a very important time to Flip It again and this time welcome support.

- **Stage 3 Acceptance:** Being able to begin accepting a loss shows that a person is starting to cope with their situation. As with each stage it doesn't happen instantly, but there are things you can do to get to this stage more quickly.

- Convey your feelings. Let yourself cry.

- Give yourself permission to feel the pain and loss.

- Get support. There are people who want to help, let them.

- Preserve as much of your lifestyle as you can. It's important to maintain a sense of security and retain some form of normality.

- Acknowledge yourself as human when you experience pain.

- Stay healthy, take care of yourself and avoid overindulgence.

- Forgive yourself for all the things you said or didn't say or do.

- Allow yourself a break from grief. You don't have to experience grief all the time to get through it.

- Get ready for anniversaries and special occasions. Decide in advance what you will do and how they will be remembered.

The loss of a loved one is quite a challenging subject to write about in a book that is positive and clearly designed to get the best out of everything. I felt it was important to write about this now, so that when the time comes (hopefully in the very distant future) when you need this information you'll be able to deal with the situation better.

I hope I've encouraged you to realise that *you can make a choice to create amazing connections that stimulate and magnify the very best of who you are*, or you can sit back and just let stuff happen.

Flip Bit

Friends and family define who we are and who we'll become.

I hope that by reading this chapter you've decided to get the very best out of all of your relationships. You'll need them as you move through life and they'll need you. That's just one of the many reasons you need to be at your very best. It's time to ...

4

Flip
It for
health

Before we start let's get a few things absolutely clear.

- I am not a doctor.
- I have no health qualifications.
- I don't have all the answers.
- I often struggle with my own weight.
- I don't know why many of the ideas in this chapter work – they just do.

I've never felt better, fitter and healthier than I do right now because of a very simple philosophy shared with me by Dr Fiona Ellis: eat well, think well, move well.

The world of health and health care is the largest and most complex field known to mankind. Trillions of pounds are provided for the health care of the sick. Billions are spent on the development of new drugs and treatments. Millions are invested in finding out why we become sick. And thousands are spent on preventing us becoming ill in the first place.

I can't help thinking if someone did some Flip It thinking with those numbers we may have a healthier society.

In this chapter I'd like to challenge a few common beliefs about health and share with you some of my discoveries in my quest for abundant vitality.

How do you feel?

Right now, as you are reading this line of Flip It, how would you describe how you are feeling? Imagine yourself standing in front of a mirror. Now how do you feel? Next imagine yourself standing on a set of scales. Now how do you feel? Unfortunately the last two feelings are how most people relate to how they feel about their health. How they look and what they weigh.

Enough has been written about why we measure our beliefs about health this way, so I'm going to let you be the judge of how you feel about that. Instead I want this chapter to be about finding wonderful ways to feel brilliant about you, your health and your well-being all the time.

Time to get healthy

OK fitness fanatics. Are you ready? I said, ARE YOU READY? Then it's time to ...

STOP, slow down, take a deep breath and relax. Did you really think I was going to suggest a programme to get you ready for a marathon in a month? This is Flip It! We do things differently around here.

I passionately believe that if you want to have a healthy body you have to start with a healthy mind. Flip It and start on the inside.

To learn how to relax properly takes the same dedication as it would to train for a marathon, it's just you will use different muscles. Many people associate relaxation with sitting in front of the TV, vegging out and generally being a bit of a slob. Whilst there is a place for that type of recreation you don't need to read a book to find out how to perfect it!

I'm challenging you to learn how to *relax properly* and, while you are in that wonderful relaxed state, to use this amazing place to programme yourself for fantastic health and vitality. That way you'll be far more inclined to do what you know you need to do, you'll find the time to do it and feel happy about the process.

Here's how to relax properly

1 Find 15 minutes. Yes you can; don't watch the news, get up 15 minutes earlier, skip a meeting. If you want to, you'll find 15 minutes.

2 Find a place where you won't be disturbed. Switch off your phone, gag your kids, etc.

3 If you are uncomfortable with silence play a relaxation CD. Could I recommend 'White Island' by Michael Heppell? It's very good.

4 Sit up. If you lie down your brain may think you are intending to have a nap, which would be nice, but not what you're looking for here.

5 Take a couple of deep breaths and close your eyes.

6 Focus on making your breathing relaxed and slow.

7 As you start to relax, focus your mind on relaxing thoughts, sounds and images.

8 As you become more and more relaxed focus your mind on the wonderful feeling of deep relaxation.

9 When your mind wanders, accept its creativity then move it back to focusing on your relaxation.

10 When you feel relaxed, take the opportunity to see yourself becoming fit and healthy. See yourself making good choices, being active and having vibrant health and energy.

11 When you feel the time is right gently count from one to five and, with each number, feel yourself becoming more alert.

12 When you reach five open your eyes, have a stretch and appreciate the feeling of being completely relaxed that you have created.

Relaxing properly takes discipline and practice. However, the rewards are brilliant. It's one of those things that we know we should do but often just don't find the time. Well what if you skipped watching the news or one of those soaps?

Deep relaxation

is one of the foundations of

vibrant health.

Time to go for that run then? Well no, not quite. Yes, getting your heart rate up is a vital part of Flip It for health but you knew that. However, I wonder if you know how important stretching is to fabulous health?

Did you know that by stretching just a few times a week you will:

● enhance your muscles;

● develop your coordination;

● increase your range of movement;

● improve your circulation;

● lubricate your joints; and

● amplify your energy levels.

Also you can do a bit of stretching, almost anywhere and, boy, is it economical!

So no running, joining a gym or spending a small fortune yet, and already you're feeling healthier and happier.

How to feel fab about flab

Disempowering beliefs about body image cause worry, anxiety and depression for many people. I too have read the articles about body image and I know perfectly well (at an intellectual level) that the guys on the front of *Men's Health* magazine are part of a tiny minority of people who have the right physiology to look like that. And yet, I could still find plenty to beat myself up about when viewing my own reflection. The challenge is when you look at yourself in a mirror what do you focus on? Exactly. You focus on what's wrong with your body.

Hmmm... nice toes

Here's a big Flip It challenge. The next time you find yourself in your birthday suit looking at your reflection I challenge you to Flip It and find three things you like about yourself. Yes it is a challenge, but a very important one.

Time to find what's right.

Flip Bit

You'll never feel fully healthy until you learn to appreciate the brilliant body you have right now.

So now is it time for a run?

Well it could be – if you had the energy.

I bet you know someone who has that uncanny (and terribly frustrating) ability to get up early and go for a five mile run before breakfast. Please stop telling the rest of us that you do it and instead share *how* you do it.

Here's what most people do when starting a 'fitness regime'. They decide to get fit – this time it's going to be different. They start on a weekend. They go for a run. They feel good. They join a gym. They have their assessment. This time it's going to be different.

Tuesday comes. They have a hell of a day. They miss a run. There's too much to do. Suddenly they haven't been to the gym for a week. They must get started again. They feel bad about their lack of commitment. They quit.

There's a key moment during that process that plots the start of the downfall and it's usually around the 'had a hell of a day' stage. *It's almost like we are subconsciously preprogrammed to find an excuse not to keep going.* When the excuse presents itself then, bingo, your subconscious was right and the downhill descent kicks in.

Next time it's going to be different.

Well if *this* **time** it *is* going to **be different** then you'd better start with a **different way of thinking**.

Here are seven Flip It ideas to make 'this time' different.

1 Have a written goal of what you want to achieve, look at it every morning and every night and visualise it clearly when you practise your relaxation.

2 Exercise your 'true will' muscle. Don't say you're going to go to the gym five days a week when the best you will manage is three. Only commit to what you know you can do and work on your 'true will' muscle alongside your others.

3 Make your commitment visual. Keep your trainers at the front door. Keep a copy of your written goal in your purse or wallet. Have your kit clean and ready to go.

4 Schedule your exercise sessions as you would any important appointments and put them in your diary. Write what you have achieved during each exercise session on a wall planner.

5 If you can afford to, get a trainer – a good one who gives a guarantee. Avoid a trainer who turns out to be a gym buddy to whom you pay good money so they can read health magazines and count your reps.

6 Create a reward system for yourself that intensely motivates you. And a punishment system that does the same.

7 Remove the word 'tired' from your vocabulary. Instead use something like, 'I could do with more energy' or 'I need to find some oomph'.

The number one reason that will stop you from exercising is believing that you are too tired, closely followed by a belief that you don't have the time. That's why it's a must to schedule time in your diary for exercise.

Another reason is, people believe it takes hours of exercise to get fit and lose weight. Not so. When I met Paul Mort of Precision Fitness my mindset changed forever. He asked me, 'Michael, how much time do you have to train'? I said it depended. If I was at home I'd have more time, but when I'm travelling, not much. Isn't that an interesting limiting belief?

Paul showed me how to Flip It by demonstrating a five-minute, full body, 'fat burning' workout you could do in a hotel room with no equipment. Then he asked, slightly sarcastically, if I could squeeze that into my 'busy schedule'.

Tired is a mindset.

No matter **how tired** you are, in **99.9 per cent**

# of cases your body still holds **enough energy** to do a **decent workout**.

Better still, after the workout you'll feel like you have an abundance of energy.

The energy creation Flip It

Here's how you can Flip It and instantly turn 'tired' into 'energetic'.

1 Accept that tired is a mindset and not a physical condition.
2 Change your language. Eliminate the word 'tired' and tell yourself you could do with more energy.
3 Start to move. Even if it's just to stand up.
4 Drink some water.
5 Put your kit on – the moment you start to get ready for exercise you will feel more energetic.
6 Tell yourself you'll start with something small. Five or ten minutes first then you'll see how you feel.
7 Start.

Quick check

You've started with the most important part – a healthy mind. You know how to relax, how to focus on the best bits to build confidence, you're clear on what you have to do to get started and you know that tired is just a mindset.

Now what to do next?

Here's the best, in my personal opinion, guide to burning fat and getting fit (based on very little medical research and shared here only because it works for me).

- **Start with something:** Anything, whatever – but start. Waiting for a gym membership, the perfect programme or a bespoke metabolic solution is just an excuse not to get active.

- **Mix it up:** I met an 80-year-old bloke who could do 200 press ups. The problem was that was all he could do. You'll meet 'experts' who claim that their way is the best or only way to get fit. I say test a load of stuff then find the things that you enjoy doing and work for you.

  In a typical week I might do one six mile run and one two mile run, a couple of Davina McCall workout DVDs (magic and my favourite) and two or three of Paul Mort's home workout fat-burning routines. If I have lots of time I'll do a 30–45-minute session, if I'm rushed I'll do 5 minutes.

- **Work with someone:** I always train with my wife. I motivate her and she certainly motivates me. Who's going to kick your butt if you decide to skip a day?

- **Stretch:** I didn't like stretching as I thought it was a waste of time. As I became fitter and my muscles grew, I found myself picking up more and more injuries. Learning how to stretch properly changed that.

- **Practise your posture:** A good posture will improve every part of your life. See an osteopath or chiropractor and ask them why.

- **Drink plenty of water:** Start the day with a 1.5-litre bottle of water and make sure you've drunk it by tea time. Exercising when dehydrated puts unnecessary strain on your body.

- **Food is 80 per cent:** As much as I've rambled about the benefit of exercise, remember that around 80 per cent of your weight gain or loss will be down to the food you eat and the liquid you drink. Damn that statistic!

Flip Bit

Isn't it amazing that even when we haven't got the time to exercise we still find the time to eat?

Dealing with illness

Feeling fit? Feeling healthy? Brilliant, time once again to Flip It and consider what to do when you're feeling unwell.

You really don't appreciate how wonderful it is to feel well until you feel ill. Some people are well all the time; others seem to get, 'everything that's going around'. Could this be a mindset? Might you actually attract illness by thinking about it?

I know a hypochondriac or two. I've noticed they all seem to have one thing in common. They get a lot of sympathy when they're unwell. In fact I noticed with one person that her kids became hypochondriacs too and, when they were unwell, like mum, they got more attention. Something to think about?

Would you agree that some people can attract sickness, others react to disease in a more adverse way and can even create illness by thinking about it?

I'm a little embarrassed to tell you this story but, many years ago, a group of colleagues and I decided to test this theory on a fellow worker. We predicted we could make her feel ill just by convincing her she wasn't well.

The set-up was simple. Everyone would comment on how poorly she looked and if she reacted we would share stories about bugs that were going around, etc. It started with the receptionist who asked if she was, 'feeling any better?' This was a stroke of genius as she hadn't even felt unwell! Over the next hour several people commented on her colour and asked if she was all right, dropping in words like sick, ill and unwell. One colleague even felt her brow and convinced her she had a temperature.

By lunchtime she was off home feeling genuinely sick, looking pale and with a temperature of 102.

If you (or others) can make you feel unwell, then if you are ill can you Flip It and make yourself

well? The simple answer is a **resounding yes**!

I once heard a brilliant reaction to a common statement when a friend of mine was obviously suffering from a heavy cold. Rather than agreeing with the diagnosis she said, 'Oh yes, I'm having a cleansing.' I don't know if she meant to say something so brilliant but it's true. When you have a cold and your nose is running, you're coughing up goodness knows what and your body feels like it's going through a medieval torture, then that's exactly what you are doing. Your body is cleansing itself of the crap that's messing it up.

I'm very fortunate as I'm always well. In fact whenever anyone starts to talk about ill health I always say that 'I'm always well', at least three times. It's a message to my subconscious and immune system and it works.

'I'm always well.'

'I'm always well.'

'I'm always well.'

But what if you do end up with an illness? Most people believe that if you're ill there's not much you can do about it other than letting time or drugs do the healing. I think you should Flip It and take on the responsibility for getting healthy again as soon as you possibly can.

Here's a list of 17 things you can do if you're unwell and want to be healthy faster.

1 **Trust yourself and listen to your body:** If your body is telling you that you need something then have it. If it's saying you shouldn't have something then don't! Sometimes your body may need a complete rest and will be telling you not to eat anything. Family and friends start to worry that 'you're not eating' and exacerbate the

situation when really you don't need food, just water. Listen to your body and trust your intuition.

2 **Remove negative emotions and stop worrying:** I appreciate this may be difficult when you're poorly, but entertaining worry and negativity is a sure fire way to hold on to your illness.

3 **Don't anticipate side-effects or pain:** Drug companies are legally obliged to inform you of any potential side-effects a medicine could have. But research has shown that, if you are told something will have a side-effect, you are actually more likely to experience it than if you didn't know. Amazing isn't it? That's how powerful your brilliant mind is. So make it work for you and decide to Flip It. Tell yourself: 'These side-effects won't affect me!'

4 **Accept that change is possible:** Some people believe that they will be stuck with pain or illness for the rest of their lives. If your body is renewing cells every minute of every day can you accept that you can change your body and ultimately how you feel?

5 **Concentrate on getting better:** It sounds very obvious but many people, when they are ill, focus on being ill and in doing so prolong the illness. When you change your focus to getting better you get better faster.

6 **Believe in your treatments:** Countless studies have shown that treatments work best when you believe they are going to work well. See your body responding well to any treatments you have to take and it will.

7 **Focus on things that give you energy:** During times when you feel unwell, your body needs to channel its energy into getting you well again. You can help it to do this by focusing on the things that give you energy. While you are resting you can still see yourself playing sport, enjoying fresh air, being on holiday, feeling vibrant, etc.

8 **Put yourself in control:** People who have experienced being very ill often comment on how they felt like 'they weren't in control'. The 'professionals' seemed to know more than they did, things happened which they didn't understand and they felt too ashamed or confused to ask.

But, you are the most important person in the world. So don't worry about feeling like a nuisance or silly. Ask all the questions you need to so you can be sure you understand what is happening. Then you can decide what is best for you. Yes, actually, you do know best! And if someone wants to change your mind they had better be very forthcoming and open with the information that will sway you.

9 **Don't focus on the pain:** Again this is a tough one but if you have pain in a particular place, then see if you can focus your mind on other parts of your body where you are pain-free. By moving your focus from the source of discomfort you can reduce the amount of pain you feel.

10 **Imagine you have a strong immune system:** Visualise your body fending off infection, see it being bold and strong. Make your thinking micro and see dodgy cells being destroyed and sickness being wiped out. Then create a brilliant defence system to keep you well. Imagine yourself as a computer and load up some antivirus software.

11 **Don't think of yourself as a sick person:** This takes us back to my friend who was 'having a cleansing'. By thinking about cleansing rather than having a cold she felt better and became healthy faster.

12 **Understand that sometimes it is all in the mind:** Your mind is amazing, but sometimes it can play some terrible tricks. Some people translate the slightest twinge into full-blown illness. By 'upgrading' your ailments like this you can seriously reduce your rate of recovery.

'Man flu' is a classic example of how a bloke can milk a cold and turn it into a near death experience. This is surpassed only by Premier League footballers who manage to display Oscar-winning pain reactions when they are tackled just inside the box. The point is, if you exaggerate how you feel you may just get what you imagined.

13 **Focus on the positive:** OK, so what's right? You've got a warm bed, people who care about you and a day off work to recover. Finding the positive – no matter how hard you have to look – will perk you up and help your recuperation. A word of warning: don't focus on finding the positives in being unwell when you're feeling well.

14 **Transform your self-talk:** Right at the start of *Flip It* I talked about the power of language. If you keep telling others (and yourself) how

unwell you are then you'll get what you focus on. Saying, 'I could be feeling better', 'I'm working on being healthy', will get you much better results.

15 **Give yourself compliments:** 'Aren't I doing well?' 'Looking good!' 'Lucky I'm such a happy soul.' 'I'm feeling better and better every day.' There are lots of good things you can say about yourself rather than looking in the mirror and saying how you 'look like crap'.

16 **Expect the best:** 'The doctor said I could be in bed for a week,' said Samantha after a home visit from her GP. A full week later she was better. I wonder how long she would have been confined to bed if her GP said she'd have to stay in bed for a couple of days.

My childhood friend Simon was told he would die before he was a teenager. This was revised to 20 after his 15th birthday. Last year he celebrated his 40th. Simon expects the best.

17 **Smile:** When you smile you give a very clear physiological message to your brain that things are good – very good. Then your brain releases the happy drugs (endorphins). These chemical neurotransmitters make it easier for you to smile and be happy. When you smile and are happy your brain releases the happy drugs and so on. Don't wait for a reason, just smile for the heck of it.

Flip Bit

'A headache is not an aspirin deficiency.' Mark Tough

Further Flip It for optimum health

My friend Mark Tough of Lifephorce says, 'A headache is certainly not an aspirin deficiency.' He's right. Our current thinking is: I feel unwell so I take something to fix it. The pharmaceutical industry is one of the biggest money makers in the world because we all want to be fixed. But what if you were to Flip It and focus on not being broken?

Is your **headache** just a **dehydration** warning?

The next time you feel a headache coming on just try drinking a large glass of water before you head for the medicine cupboard. If you find yourself getting headaches on a regular basis then dramatically reduce the amount of caffeine you consume and significantly increase the amount of water you drink.

One of my greatest discoveries as a brilliant health fix came when I found a new way to treat indigestion. I used to suffer almost every day and in an attempt to treat the pain scoffed all sorts of indigestion tablets. That was until I had a brilliant Flip It moment and discovered apple cider vinegar. The chances are that you will be thinking, as I did, that the last thing I would want to take whilst suffering from indigestion is apple cider vinegar.

Just in case you are reading this bit without reading the warning at the beginning, I am not a doctor; I have no health qualifications and my theory as to why this works is purely speculation. But if you suffer from indigestion, acid reflux, heartburn or whatever they are calling it at the moment then you may want to try this. As soon as you feel any pain just take one teaspoon of organic apple cider vinegar and in seconds all discomfort has gone.

My simple-minded theory as to why this works is that your body is trying to produce extra acid to compensate for whatever else you have put into it in the hours before. As soon as you take the apple cider vinegar your brilliant body says, 'OK, we have enough acid now. No more acid is needed.'

I've since found out that good old apple cider vinegar has other health benefits too, but I'll leave you to research those for yourself.

Flip It for Health could be 90 per cent of this book, but I'm running out of pages to share everything I want to share with you. I've barely got the space to suggest you stop thinking about yourself getting old and frail, Flip It and imagine yourself growing older and stronger.

Even some of the simple Flip It ideas, like moving your car's rear-view mirror up a little so you have to sit up straight to use it and in the process improve your posture may take too much explaining.

Flip It for health is designed to inspire you into action and to do some (or some more) of the simple things to have a vibrant healthy life. Here's to being flippin' healthy!

Given the choice of health or wealth, which would you choose? The Flip It answer is you can have both! Time to dive in to ...

5

Flip It for money

Success can be measured by many things. Some measure it by the amount of money they have. Although I don't fully subscribe to that, I do believe one measure of success is your ability to make money and create wealth.

Pay yourself first

The more I study happy prosperous people the more I realise they use Flip It thinking to acquire their wealth. It starts with a simple mindset that the wealthy have called 'pay yourself first'.

When I first discovered 'pay yourself first' I became very excited as I thought it meant I would take a percentage of my income every month before paying any bills and use it first to buy myself treats and make me feel good. I was half right. Yes you do take a percentage of your income each month before you pay anyone else but you save the money. *Every month, month in month out, without fail.*

If you are reading this and you currently earn exactly enough to pay your monthly bills you'll probably be thinking, 'When I earn more, then I'll save', or 'When I've paid off more of my debts, then I'll save'. If that's you then *you need to Flip It right now and create a new belief system if you want to be wealthy.*

I really believe that the vast majority of people who spend all they earn could use this simple system to get started on the road to prosperity.

- **Step 1** Find ways to cut back on your expenditure by at least 10 per cent.
- **Step 2** Find the right type of savings account for you.
- **Step 3** Set up a standing order to pay a percentage (10 per cent is a good start) into your savings account the day you get paid.
- **Step 4** Review after a year and see if you can afford to save more.
- **Step 5** Reinvest the interest.

I'm pretty certain at this point that many readers will have a challenge with Step 1. Most people are not taught good financial management skills; we have lived with an attitude of spend now and pay for it later. This is fine when you can control the payments and you are using OPM (other people's money) to leverage your goals but in many cases it's just that we think we need the things we don't.

Flip Bit

Have you noticed how close the words need and greed are to each other?

My friend Chris was always a very good spender. One day (I think it was his 50th birthday) he got it into his head that he was going to be a saver. He went nuts and within a few months had saved a small fortune. When I asked him what he had done differently he said it was all simple stuff, 'I just made my mind up to do things differently.'

What Chris did was to Flip It from excessive to thrifty. One of my favourite pieces of Flip It thinking he tested was around cash. Chris loved to carry a wad of cash. When he became a saver he made the decision to leave the house with just £1 in his pocket.

It's **amazing** what you *can't* **buy** when you only have £1.

There are lots of other ways to find the 10 per cent. From buying cheaper brands, eating out less, renegotiating bills, deferring a holiday, preparing your own lunch, etc. You know what to do – but now it's time to do it.

Do this and you'll have the mindset of a saver. Now it's time to look at how to make more money. So you can save more not spend it!

Let's make lots of money

People who have made a lot of money usually say they have one of two mindsets. The first is that they didn't set out to make money and the financial success is just a by-product of what they did. The second is that they had a goal to earn a certain amount of money then they set out to earn it. You choose which one works best for you – but choose you must.

Most people don't have any strategy or written goals about how much money they want to earn. Coincidently most people don't believe they are earning enough either!

Unfortunately the only tactic they have is based around a misguided belief that they are owed a living or that if they were paid more then they would do more. They hope to win the lottery. Sound familiar? If that's you then you'd better sit down as I have some very bad news for you. It is incredibly unlikely to happen – especially the lottery bit.

The making money Flip It

It's that time once again to Flip It and start to ask better questions. Here are three simple ones.

- What can I do to make more money now?
- How can I add more value?
- What resources do I have?

When it comes to resources I think you'll be surprised just what is available to you. Here's a simple audit you can do for yourself. Tick every box that applies to you.

- I have the use of a computer. ☐
- I have more than 10 friends. ☐
- I could work harder. ☐
- I can be creative. ☐
- I watch TV for more than four hours per week. ☐
- I can make things. ☐
- I have transport. ☐
- I am open-minded. ☐
- I am prepared to work hard. ☐
- I have £50 I could spend on my education. ☐

How many of those statements describe you?

Brilliant that's the most important bit done. The idea that you can make money needs to be set in stone before you will make money.

Brilliant you've got a list of your resources. Time to start to flex your confidence muscles in the money-making department.

Now be clear in the task of making some money. For some this may be a little extra to clear a debt or pay for a treat, for others it could be total financial security. Write it down, right now, how much extra income you want to make in the next 12 months.

> **Flip Bit**
>
> You get what you think about the most. Think about how little you have and you could end up with less. Focus on the amazing resources you have now, the value you can add and the numerous ways you can make more and money will be attracted to you.

Next it's all about the action. You do know that to make money you have to take action – don't you?

Owing lots of money

How can this ever be a good thing? Owing lots of money can be stressful, tiring and lead to challenges in relationships, work and health. In an ideal world you wouldn't owe too much money and the debts you do have would be managed easily. Unfortunately this is not an ideal world.

Many people find themselves owing just too much. If that's you then I hope *Flip It* can help. This is just a short section with a couple of simple ideas; many more can be found in specialist books, at advice centres, etc. But as you're here let's Flip It and get the best out of this situation by using a watery metaphor.

- **Step 1   Money is an energy:** Create a belief that money is just energy, which means it's going to flow in and flow out of your life – like water. I guess the challenge you've had is that it's been flowing out a little faster than it's been flowing in.

- **Step 2   Build a dam:** A money dam is designed to hold on to as much money as it can. Yes, some might leak through, but your job is to make sure every crack is filled and every hole plugged. This involves getting brilliantly organised, knowing exactly what you're doing with your money and making a plan. It also means you won't waste money – did you know that on average we each spend around £4,000 on impulse purchases each year? Now that's food for thought as you are reaching for that chocolate bar at the newsagents.

- **Step 3 Create a monsoon:** One of the challenges of owing lots of money is the belief that the money flow will stop – it won't. So be open to the possibility that more money will flow in and believe you deserve it. This mindset is vital.

- **Step 4 Get some quick wins:** If you had to fill a glass, a bucket, and a bath which one would you fill first? Correct. You'd fill the glass first. By getting a quick win and paying off a small debt you'll start to create momentum which will accelerate your success.

- **Step 5 Keep a record:** As you go through this process keep a diary of each stage, what you've done and how you feel. This journal will be an inspiration to you later and you'll be surprised and delighted at what you have achieved in a relatively short period of time.

- **Step 6 Make it work for you:** Water is all around and yet we buy it. Why? Because the people who know how to supply it hold the power. When you have paid your debts, learn how to make money work for you.

Flip It for investing

Many people waste time and waste money then blame others for the situation they got themselves into. I bet you are more pleased than ever that you're not most people. The idea of any investment is to get a return.

Here are a few simple truths to consider about investing before you start.

- **Truth 1:** Remember, becoming a great investor is not about levels of income, it starts with your attitude towards money.

- **Truth 2:** If you want to be a financial investor, learn from those who have always been investors. The first thing you'll notice is they always find a way to invest, even if it's just a small amount – investing money is a mindset first.

- **Truth 3:** Be comfortable with your level of risk. As a rule of thumb, think like this: if it's as 'safe as houses' you'll feel comfortable but won't earn so much. If it looks too good to be true, that's almost certainly because it is!

- **Truth 4:** Remember, money is an energy that flows – it flows in and flows out. And always will.

- **Truth 5:** There will always be someone whose investments are earning more than yours, someone who spotted a trend before you did and who can invest much more than you can. Good for them.

- **Truth 6:** There are exceptions to rules one to five.

Most people can save, but few choose to invest either for one or a combination of these reasons.

1 Don't know how to.

2 Fear of failure.

3 Believe they haven't got enough money to invest.

Why invest?

Can't you just get stuff on a credit card or borrow from a bank? Well yes you can but it's a sure-fire way to end up in financial ruin, as we so deftly proved in 2008 with sub-prime loans, overextending, and some decidedly dodgy strategies from the guys at the top.

If you don't have the knowledge now you can learn it!

Right now you can go on investment courses, join clubs and learn online. There are dozens of excellent books available on how to invest so I'm sure you'll find the right thing for you. Yes you'll make mistakes but, seriously, could you get it any more wrong than some of the mighty institutions that are supposed to 'know' about investing?

Fear of failure

Investment can seem very daunting and many fear the risks are too great. So they create a belief system that they shouldn't start until they get more: knowledge, cash, until the market is right, etc.

Of course, in reality, investment – if approached in the right way – needn't be high risk at all. Here's an idea to get you started and to help you overcome that fear.

Imagine you have three barrels which are standing one on top of each other. The top barrel is your easy access barrel, which is used for day-to-day living expenses. Your second barrel is for safe investments. And the third (bottom) barrel is your higher-risk investments.

Your job is to fill the barrels from top to bottom. In the top barrel (the one that gives you easy access), you need to have enough money stored to pay for three months' worth of expenses. This is basic saving, really.

So if you have a lifestyle that costs £1,000 per month you need £3,000 in that barrel. It's fair to say that if you don't have any current investments then that may seem like a huge stretch, and not a very sexy one, as you'll be putting your money into an easy access building society or bank account or perhaps maximising a tax-efficient government incentive to save.

However, once you have filled that barrel, any excess will start to pour over into your second barrel. This includes the money you were putting into the first barrel prior to filling it, plus the interest the first barrel produces. This barrel should be built to hold the equivalent of 6 to 12 months' salary. This can be deposited in safer investments such as blue-chip companies with excellent steady growth records, property and legitimate investment schemes.

Finally your third barrel will start to fill with the overflow from the success of barrel number two. You can use this to further invest in the areas from barrel two or you can take some higher-risk investment opportunities. And here's the exciting bit – you get to spend what overflows from barrel three!

It may take you many years to fill all three barrels but the most important thing is to make a start. If you don't do it now you will kick yourself later.

Invest and invest again

When your investments start to pay, the real key is to reinvest the interest. It will be tempting to take the interest and spend it. You'll say things like, 'Haven't I done well, I deserve it.' It's tough, but every great investor used the same formula of reinvesting their returns to create highly successful investment portfolios.

Here's why: two magic words – *compound interest*.

Did you know that if you invested £1,000 now, with an annual return of 8 per cent you would have £46,902 in 50 years? That may seem like a long time (and a very high rate until you contemplate what you can achieve in those 50 years!)

However, what if you could Flip It and become a brilliant investor? What if you invested £5,000 over 30 years with a 20 per cent return? You've just made a million!

The younger you are the more time you can take. You can afford to make some gaffes but in time you'll also get a bigger return.

How much is enough?

If many people believe they need more money before they can start to invest, how much is enough – £100, £1,000, £10,000? Well, I really do believe you can start to learn about investing with as little as £200.

It's actually more about getting started than waiting until you have 'enough'. And when you do have enough you won't want to risk losing it by making the wrong investments if you have no experience.

'Rule No.1: Never lose money. Rule No. 2: Never forget Rule No.1.'

Warren Buffett

Financial security is great, but it's only one way to look at success.

Real achievement can be measured in many ways – that's why I wrote a special section called ...

6

Flip
It for
success

We often tend to disguise our faults and hope people won't discover them. Let's Flip It so the opposite is true. Flip It thinking suggests you can use faults and foibles in a positive way and, potentially, they could become the secret of your success.

Turning faults into fortunes

What's your thing? Too tall, too small, fat or thin? Perhaps you think you are too old, too young or your teeth are too big?

By learning how to get the best out of these perceived negatives you'll not only feel better about them but you'll also quickly realise they offer some distinct benefits.

I once interviewed a very tall lad for a job. He was a semi-professional basketball player and at almost seven feet tall he had quite a presence. He knew his career in basketball was limited and wanted to know if he had a chance in sales. Unfortunately, as soon as he walked into the room, he looked as if he was almost apologising for his height.

After a while he brought up his tallness and suggested it might be a problem. 'No way,' I said, 'in fact it's a huge positive.' 'You could use it as an ice-breaker,' I suggested. 'Why not say, "before I used Michael Heppell's techniques I was just five foot six".'

Granted, this may not have been one of my best ideas, but the point is he was too close to his best asset, his amazing height. I knew he could use it as an asset but unfortunately he chose to see it as a fault.

Here's a Flip It for success challenge. Take the part of you that you think of as your greatest fault and ask how you can Flip It and use it for success? It won't work every time but you'll be surprised by your change of thinking around your perceived faults.

Take a break – break the rules

Don't walk on the grass! OK, but what happens if you do? A friend of mine encourages his kids to walk on the lawns when he sees 'Keep off the grass' signs. Irresponsible? Maybe, but his argument is he wants his kids to break some rules so they don't feel like they always have to do what they are told is 'right'. He wants them to make their own minds up and have the confidence in later life to say no to drugs, etc. even if they find themselves in a room full of mates who are all taking something.

Studying successful people often leads you to realise that they too tend to break a few rules along the way to get different results. Flip It thinking here doesn't necessarily mean turning it around 180 degrees. In fact, a slight shift may be all you need to get some fantastically different results.

In January 2005 Chad Hurley wanted to send some videos he and some friends made at a dinner party to the other guests. Emails were rejected because of the file size and embedding video on websites was difficult. Not only that but he would have had to share passwords and log ins. Hurley decided to beak a rule and create an easy video uplink that anyone could see. This method became popular and his crazy idea took off. Less than two years later he sold his company *YouTube* to Google for $1.65 billion.

What **don't you do** because of your fear of **breaking the rules**?

The breaking rules Flip It

Before you read any further, I won't accept any responsibly for using this technique and getting some unplanned results, but I will encourage you to flex your risk muscle. Here are a few to get you started.

- Do change times. What if your working day was different?
- Don't watch the news (especially the local news) for a month.
- Don't recruit on psychometric tests. Try likeability first.
- Do miss a deadline (by asking for an extra day).
- Don't drink when everyone else is getting smashed.
- Do cook without a recipe.
- Do smile more often.
- Do walk on the grass.

Flip Bit

Breaking rules has consequences but so does sticking with them. By breaking the right rules at the right time you can uncover some amazing hidden successes.

The cure to procrastination

I'm world class at procrastination. If it were an Olympic event I'm sure I could bring home gold for Britain – even though I'd probably be delayed picking up the medal. When you are as naturally good at procrastinating as I am, you need a few tools and techniques up your sleeve to get past the big P or you just wouldn't get anything done.

Using Flip It is a brilliant way to overcome procrastination, get things done and be more successful at the same time.

My first tool is maybe a little wayward for some readers, so stick with me. Basically it's to tell a lovely lie. But when I say lie, I mean lie in a nice 'little white' way. Lie in a way which, when done correctly, ensures you feel motivated to take action – mainly so you won't get caught out.

Come on, you've done it at one time or another. Perhaps you said you'd tidied up, hadn't, then had to rush off home for a dust and clear. Or you said you had made that important call, then immediately made the call you'd just sworn you'd already completed (we've all done that one!)

I think one of the reasons we let procrastination beat us is because of the importance we give it. Let me explain. There are several types of procrastination.

- Not doing anything.
- Doing the wrong thing.
- Working on something more important.

If you are working on something more important than what may appear to be urgent then procrastination can be a good thing.

Richard Hamming was a mega researcher who worked for many years for Bell Laboratories. He got things done, won countless awards and changed the world we live in. Rather than trying to get everything done he would Flip It by suggesting all you need to do to overcome procrastination is to ask three simple questions.

1 What are the most important problems in your field?
2 Are you working on one of them?
3 Why not?

That's one of those so devastatingly simple formulas that you need to read it couple of times. Don't procrastinate, read it a couple of times – do it now!

> **Flip Bit**
> What's the best thing you could be working on and why aren't you?

Making deadlines deadly

Another way to overcome procrastination is to set outrageous deadlines. Dave is a film maker, and a very good one. But he procrastinates; he makes excuses about being busy, complains that he has problems with clients, etc. However, he'll always hit a deadline. Often he tells me during his rants that there are 24 hours in a day and if necessary he can use all of them.

Dave makes many of our training and promotion films and knowing how Dave works gives me an advantage. I always shrink the deadline by a couple of days. This means if something does go wrong there's always an opportunity to fix it before the real deadline.

Here's the weird thing. Dave knows I do that but he still often ends up working all night to complete a piece of work to meet the earlier deadline. Why? Dave has a strong desire to please.

After discussing this with him he now uses his desire to please as his own driver as a way to self-motivate. He'll ask clients, 'When do you need this done by?' and if they say 'The 15th', he'll throw in, 'I'll see if I can get it done by the 12th'.

How could you **shrink your deadlines** to encourage you to **get things done**?

Flip Bit

Of authors, 98 per cent (including this one) complete their manuscript on the last day of their contract deadline. Make a commitment – and it gets done.

Rock to resolution

If I were to tell you that your biggest problems are actually the keys to your greatest successes, what would you think? And rightly so!

But let me challenge that thinking. I really do believe that problems are a gift. The more you have the more you're doing, the bigger the problems the bigger the reward!

I worked for someone who frequently used to throw out the old cliché, 'We don't have problems – just opportunities'. There were days when I could have strung him up. Of course we have problems! Then he came back from a two-day management course and announced, 'We don't have problems we only have solutions.'

That was the tipping point for me. I listed three major problems and asked how on earth they could be thought of as solutions. He then systematically showed me how each of my problems was in fact an opportunity to do something creative and different and that there was a solution for each of them. It was time for me to eat a hefty slice of humble pie.

Over the years I drifted in and out of this way of thinking until I realised that, as a procrastinator who needs simple tried and tested ideas that work (and work fast), I needed a tool to utilise this type of thinking.

Rock to resolution was created.

Here's how it works.

- **Step 1:** This is the easy part as it involves identifying your rock. The rock is the big issue, which seems to be holding you back, causing a problem or putting you in a predicament. You'll probably already have a good idea what the rock is. Write this clearly in the 'rock box'.

- **Step 2:** Break down the rock into specific problems. It doesn't matter how many but the more it's broken down the easier it is to find your solutions. Write each individual challenge in the 'problem column'.

- **Step 3:** Take each problem and write down a simple solution in the solution column. You don't have to know all the how to's at this point but make sure there is a brief note next to each problem.

- **Step 4:** Read your list of solutions and think how it would feel if you had all of those solutions in place. Then write the resolution in the box.

If you are into goal setting you may wish to write a target date beneath the resolution to encourage you to take early action.

Rock to Resolution

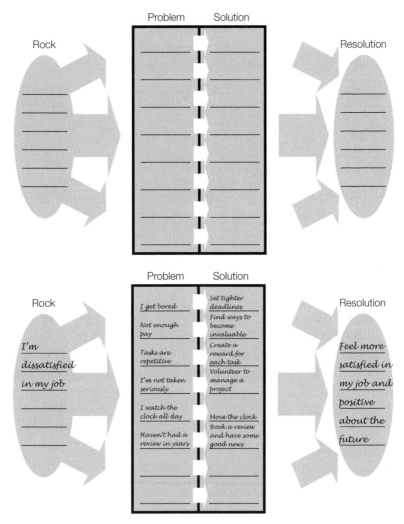

Rock to resolution is a very powerful tool that works best if you write everything down. You can download Rock to resolution templates from my website: www.michaelheppell.com

Stop listening to bad advice!

Have you noticed that as we grow older we focus more and more on what we can't do rather than what we can? Here's a question. Hands up if you're good at art? Having asked the question of thousands of people, I know that only 3 in 100 readers will believe they are actually good at art.

Now take your mind back to when you were five years old. You're in a school assembly and the headteacher says, 'Hands up if you are good at art'. At that point what happens? Correct, all hands shoot up in the air.

So what happened between five and now? The simple answer is 11. Yes good old 11 happened. At around 11 years old you went to 'big school'. One day you were sitting in art focusing vigorously on your 2B pencil drawing of some carefully arranged fruit. Then mid flow, just as you were delicately shading a banana's soft shadow on a plump plum, your best mate stood over your shoulder, gestured at your work and said 'That's shit.'

And you believed them!

I bet you wish you had the confidence then that you do now so you could Flip It and throw back a witty retort along the lines of, 'No it's not actually, this is my brilliant impressionist view of that fruit.' But unfortunately you didn't. You looked at the page and thought, yes it is pretty crappy isn't it?

But now you know differently, don't you? Don't you? Actually, no you don't. *You still believe what people say when they give you poor feedback.* You take it to heart and make it personal.

Often we react to negative feedback in a negative way. When this happens it creates a 'lose/lose' situation. What if you were to Flip It and think about negative feedback with the same mindset as when you receive Marks & Spencer presents?

I'll explain. It's your birthday. Now imagine your aunt/mum/brother or whoever is eagerly waiting for you to unwrap their nicely gift-wrapped present. You open it and there nestled in the wrapping paper is *the jumper from hell* – wrong colour/pattern/batwings … just awful. Just when your fake smile is about to crack you spot the label, 'Marks & Spencer'. Suddenly faking gratitude is easy because you know that now you have choice: you can take the jumper from hell back to good old M&S and exchange it for something you will like or, even better, cash!

The feedback Flip It

The next time you're faced with this situation where someone wants to give you 'feedback' here's the Flip It way to think about it.

- Smile and say 'thank you'.
- Ask them if they really meant what they said.
- Wait a few minutes.
- Ask yourself if there was any validity in what they said.
- Ask yourself if acting on their comment will really help to make you better.

Sometimes people don't give feedback well, or they don't actually mean what they say and don't for a second consider the consequences.

The next time you **get feedback** that **isn't helpful** remember, you have a **choice**.

If you don't want it then just imagine that you can return it to the shop. I don't mean literally say to someone 'I don't want that feedback'. But you can say a polite 'thank you' then decide that it is not useful or relevant for you and choose not to take it on board.

Flip Bit

Do you eat everything you see? No? Then don't believe everything you hear.

Eliminating your 'I've quit' gestures

I've recently coached a couple of people from the wonderful world of sport. Watching a video of one of my clients I noticed the exact moment in a game when he quit. He had gestures, mannerisms and a distinct physiology which demonstrated that he'd quit the game long before the final whistle.

Before you become my dad and start to shout about how overpaid sports people are and how they quit too soon, etc, think about your own 'I've quit' gestures and ask how they may be affecting your game.

We all have certain gestures that we associate with quitting a task. Exasperated arms, shaking heads and some none too friendly profanities are amongst them.

Take a moment to consider what you do when you quit. Do you:

shake your head;	throw things;	grit your teeth;
fold your arms;	tut;	walk away;
say 'no';	look down;	swear.
exhale sharply;	scream;	
slap your forehead;	shrug;	
pull your hair;	put your hands over your eyes.	

Now what if you were to Flip It and take a moment to consider what you do when you feel super successful.

make a fist;	stand up;
say 'yes';	shout;
smile;	do a little dance;
thumbs up;	nod your head;
punch the air;	pout your lips;
look up;	jump from side to side.

Congratulations! You have joined a very small percentage of people who are actually aware of their 'I've quit' and 'I'm a success' gestures.

What would happen if, during a time when you felt very successful, you started to repeatedly use your 'I've quit' gestures? It wouldn't take long before you were sliding down the spiral of negativity and landing with a nasty bump.

So if that's the case, wouldn't it make sense that now you are aware of your 'I've quit' gestures, if you find yourself in that unresourceful state, you could repeatedly use your 'I'm a success' gestures to Flip It and flip out of that pessimistic place?

Here's a challenge. The next time you catch yourself using 'I've quit', gestures say the words 'Flip It' and replace what you are doing with the opposite 'I'm a success' gesture. You'll be amazed and surprised by the instant results!

By playing with your physiology like this you'll be able to flip your emotional state very quickly. You'll feel better faster and attract success.

Act like the meerkat – heads up!

Don't you just love the meerkat? He sits with his head up tall searching for opportunities to feed and predators to avoid. The meerkat survives because it takes action.

Most people move through life with their heads down and complain later when they missed an opportunity. If you adopt the meerkat 'heads up' approach you'll spot multiple opportunities for success.

The best bit is, by looking for opportunities like this, with an open mind, each opportunity spotted often leads to another. It gets easier.

Brilliant opportunity is all around but sometimes we need to Flip It and change views to fully grasp what's available.

You may have been taught that successful people are very 'single-minded'. I disagree. Most successful people I meet are open to many views and ways of thinking. Consciously or not they use a technique called reframing. This simply means you are able to look at things from several points of view.

There are many uses for this skill but, when it's combined with a 'heads up' approach, reframing gives you very powerful results.

Change your view – become a master reframer

By learning how to see multiple viewpoints you immediately see solutions that were hiding behind a traditional one-dimensional outlook.

What do you do when you have one shot at promoting your business to your most influential customer? Five-star service is the minimum expectation, along with a whole host of boxes to tick.

When the Milestone Hotel in Kensington, London, was faced with this challenge they decided to Flip It. By looking closely at what Amex customers wanted, the team at the Milestone quickly discovered there was a lot of competition for the normal five-star offering, so they reframed their meeting with Amex and asked them a brilliant question: 'If there was one commodity you could provide for your customers that money could not buy, what would it be?' Their answer was 'time'.

That's when the Milestone created a unique package for Amex guests, 'The 24-hour stay'. No matter what time you arrive the room is yours for 24 hours. Imagine being able to check in at 6 pm and leave at 6 pm the next day? No rushing to check out, no storing of bags. Perfect.

What challenge can you **Flip It**, reframe, approach with a heads up view and get amazing results?

Chunky and sautéed elephants

Question: How do you eat an elephant?

Answer: A bite at a time!

Old joke, not particularly funny and often used to describe overcoming a large task.

Now let's bring it up to date and add some Flip It thinking.

Question: How do you eat an elephant?

Answer: Sautéed, with a mild curry sauce, lots of fresh spring vegetables, a couple of glasses of a deliciously chilled Sauvignon Blanc and don't forget to invite a few friends round – chances are they won't have tried sautéed elephant.

Remember with Flip It you can get the very *best* out of any given situation. So if your task was to eat an elephant, why would you want to do it a bite at a time when it could be a fabulous feast with friends?

Let's use the chunky method for one of the most exciting tasks we have to do – the housework!

- **Step 1   Make a list:** Isn't it funny how big tasks are more manageable when they're turned into lists? Plus, as you achieve each part of the task, it feels fab when you add a giant tick.

- **Step 2   Create a reward system for yourself:** Here's what we normally do, 'I'll have a cup of tea and then I'll get started'. *No!* Have your cup of tea after the vacuuming.

- **Step 3   Turn the music up:** It's always easier to do housework with great music. If you have an iPod, create a happy housework playlist.

- **Step 4   Add smells:** As you complete a room, finish by spraying a nice scent. Your desk feels cleaner with the smell of polish, a loo feels fresh with a nice de-pong … you get the idea.

- **Step 5   Set a target time:** If you think you can get everything done in three hours, then set the time and go for beating it. You may want to add a reward for every 10 minutes you beat it by.

Any task can be made more manageable and enjoyable by creatively chunking it in to tasty bite-sized pieces.

Developing your intuition

What happens when you flip a coin to make a decision? Hundreds of thoughts fly through your mind from the moment the coin leaves your hand to the final reveal of a head or tail. Hidden in these messages is the actual result you really want.

If I am working with someone who can't make their mind up between A and B I say, 'OK let's flip a coin.' We then decide, heads it's A and tails it's B. Then I flick the coin making sure it's spinning vigorously. As soon as I catch it, I cover it up and ask them quickly, 'Which one did you want it to be?' and 90 per cent of the time they'll respond. At that point I put the coin in my pocket and never reveal which side it actually landed on.

When you know – you know.

If you learn how to develop this intuitive thinking then you won't need to flip it again – the coin that is.

Flip Bit
Why chance luck when you can depend on intuition?

Intuition is a master skill that needs to be developed through use. Have you ever been in one of those situations where, after an unusual event occurs, you just knew it was going to happen? How did you know?

Experience, subconscious, unique ability all play a part. The challenge is we often only realise our intuition was talking to us after the event. Think of your intuition as an associate who is there with you all the time. The only challenge is this partner doesn't always speak the same language as you. In fact sometimes your partner doesn't speak at all, preferring to mime a message or draw clues. The challenge is if you choose to ignore these messages and clues then you won't ever get any better at reading them.

The Trusted Translator

Now imagine you have a tiny translator who is sitting on your shoulder whispering in your ear. You trust your translator as they always give you good advice, so let's call them your Trusted Translator.

The more you use your Trusted Translator the better you get at understanding your intuition and what it's really telling you.

Here are three ways to develop your Trusted Translator.

1   **Listen to that hunch:** I taught a leadership programme to the

High Performance Officers Scheme of the Metropolitan Police. One day we ended up talking about individual safety. I asked a seasoned officer about the best way to increase personal protection. His response was fascinating. He said, 'You know that feeling that you get when you're walking down the street and you just know you shouldn't be there? Well, listen to it as you're absolutely right – you shouldn't.'

That's your intuition talking. You can't see anything and there is no logical reason why something should be wrong but listening to that hunch could be the best move you ever make.

2   **Make it real:** Who do you trust? What if you were to make your Trusted Translator that person? You could have more than one if you'd like a range of opinions to consider, but ensure you trust them all. The next time you need to tap in to your intuition simply close your eyes, visualise your Trusted Translator(s) and listen to what's said.

3   **Turn it into a question:** Sometimes our intuition needs a prompt. By turning how we are feeling into a question it's amazing how often the right answer pops up. Here are a few to get you started.

- Why am I feeling this?
- What action should I take next?
- How can I handle this for the best results?
- What's best for all concerned?
- What should I do next?

If you write the question down this technique seems to be even more effective.

By **developing your intuition** you'll quickly find decision making easier, you'll **trust your**

judgement and find challenges you face **easier to deal with**.

Flip it for success is the most challenging and rewarding chapter in this book. It favours the brave and those who are prepared to turn the ideas into actions.

I'm now challenged with what to write to link this chapter with the next. I know what I need, it's ...

7

Flip It for creativity

Perhaps one of the most exciting things about creativity is that it can be learned. Combine this with the fact that creative people earn more, do more and are generally more successful in every area of life and you've got a pretty compelling reason to read this chapter.

As you've probably spotted by now Flip It is all about creativity and the art of thinking differently. The essence of this book is about turning ideas on their heads, stretching boundaries and doing things another way. I love the idea of challenging 'conventional' wisdom.

So how creative are you? Here's a little test.

Tick the following statements that apply to you.

1 You love using colour. ☐
2 You like to know where everything is. ☐
3 You see more than one correct answer. ☐
4 You like deadlines. ☐
5 You learn from mistakes. ☐
6 You tend to 'go with the flow'. ☐
7 You're happy to be out on a limb. ☐
8 You don't like making mistakes. ☐
9 You contribute a lot during brainstorms. ☐
10 You are a 'completer finisher'. ☐
11 You see answers when others see problems. ☐
12 You like a system. ☐

If you've ticked all odd numbers then you're very creative and probably a bit of a nightmare to live and work with.

If you've ticked only even numbers then creativity is alien to you and I bet your favourite colour is grey!

It's more likely that you'll have a slight majority of either the odd or even ticks. As my goal isn't to make you less analytical (it's to make you more creative) we're just going to focus on adding to your creative side.

Break a routine

One of the easiest ways to start being more creative is to break a routine. When we become creatures of habit we miss out on new thoughts, creativity and the opportunity to innovate.

Time to Flip It and break some of your most common routines.

> I can't guarantee that you will instantly become **more creative** by doing this but I can guarantee that **something will happen**.

Ivan had lived in the same house for 22 years. He had worked for the same company for 15 years and completed a 45-minute commute to and from work every day. That was until Ivan was forced to break his routine. A new pipeline was being laid and his route to work would be blocked for five days. Ivan was forced to make a detour.

The first day Ivan, like the majority of commuters, complained, raised his blood pressure and blamed the contactors for a thoroughly stupid detour. Then something different happened on day two.

Ivan found himself sitting in slow-moving traffic, casually looking out of his car window when he spotted an old barn with a 'For Sale' sign attached to it. 'Who'd buy an old barn like that?' he thought.

On his way home that evening he found himself studying the old barn with a little more than a passing interest.

On day three he pulled over and found himself looking round the old place. He took the number of the estate agent, called them and requested the details.

By day four a plan was forming.

Day five and tragedy struck. The road had reopened a day earlier than had been expected. What should have been a happy occasion was tainted for Ivan by overefficient pipe layers! No drive by the aged barn for Ivan.

However, that weekend he arranged to view the old barn and on Monday morning he made an offer. Ivan spent every spare moment of the next two years working on his new project – a barn conversion.

The results were amazing. The use of space, the natural light, the innovation and the quality were all admired by visitors.

When Ivan moved into his new home it also became his office. You see, Ivan was an architect who, for the last 15 years, had drawn plans for positioning ATMs on the walls of banks. His imagination had lain dormant. Ivan's creativity just needed a kick-start.

Ivan gets his inspiration from all over the place now, often taking a wrong turn just to see where he ends up.

Which routine could you Flip in search of inspiration? Here are a few ideas to get you started.

The breaking routines Flip Its

Have a big night out … on a Monday.
Go somewhere cold for your holidays.
Turn right and see where you end up.
Get into work at 7 am.
Swap desks.
Eat a backwards meal – start with dessert.
If you read a daily newspaper buy a very different one.
Get the train, bus or plane.
Watch an alternative movie.
Dress up – or dress down.
Change your *font type*, size or colour.

When you break routines it's also worth raising your level of awareness. You can do this by holding 'conscious self-talk'. By this I mean being more aware of your internal dialogue. When you notice something, rather than getting frustrated say to yourself, 'That's interesting, how can I: use this, adapt it, make it work for me, etc.

This method of self-analysis is quite different from our usual thought process, which tends to allow thoughts to drift in and out, possibly without getting the most from them.

Allow yourself the luxury of **daydreaming** some possibilities.

You can see children thinking this way when they come across a new concept to consider, problem to solve or idea to comprehend. It's clear on their faces and you can even hear as they ask themselves in whispers questions about what's happening.

Think like a child

What if you were to Flip It and think more like a child?

Children think differently. They also learn faster, test out more ideas and have more fun. Not a bad way to think. Kids are encouraged at an early age to explore, take risks and go for it. Later as they grow older this gets knocked out of them by a combination of the school system and peer pressure. It's tragic to see how little creativity many older teenagers leave school with compared to the magical open-minded toddlers who joined the system.

Here's a challenge for you. The next time you have a problem you need to fix, tackle it in the same way a child would.

And if you've forgotten what children do to learn then here are some ideas.

- **Pick it up:** Kids love to touch stuff. Adults try to fix 90 per cent of their problems through a Google search.
- **Turn it into a game:** You learn more when you're playing – much more. How can you turn your problem into a game?

- **Add colour:** Have you seen the bright magical colours of a nursery? Now compare that to your office. Colour improves the activity levels in the receptors of your brain.

- **Draw:** Get a big pad, lots of coloured pens and start to draw. Learn how to mindmap and think in pictures.

- **Leave it when you get fed up:** Kids know when to stop. It's at the exact same time that their interest starts to shut down. So they find something else to do and then go back to the problem later, with renewed energy.

- **Ask stupid questions:** Adults get embarrassed when asking the daft question. Kids thrive on it! What daft questions could you ask, who to and how often?

What **benefits** could there be if you **thought** like a child?

The real beauty of thinking like a child is that as an adult you can (and have to) switch it on and off.

Consider this, the next time you have a problem you could: think like a child for 10 minutes, get the solution, then spend the next 50 minutes doing a full cost analysis, time-frame projection and cross-departmental resource breakdown. Try doing that when you're five!

Flip Bit

Children have the luxury of thinking like children all the time.

How would nature deal with this?

I was conducting a brainstorming session with a group of school principals, looking into methods for improving levels of achievement. During the brainstorm I asked, 'How would a teacher deal with this?' To which one of the participants commented, 'It would become extinct.'

I, along with the rest of the room, must have looked very confused as we gazed at him in silence. 'Well that's how *nature* would deal with it', he explained. He misheard 'nature' for 'teacher' and inadvertently created one of the best questions to ask in a creative brainstorming session, 'How would nature deal with this?'

Since then I've used this question hundreds of times. If your relationship wasn't working would nature make it extinct? Or have it evolve? Could your product be made poisonous to predators? Where might you find nourishment if a regular food source ran out?

Nature is the most ingenious, resourceful and adaptable force known to mankind. By asking how nature would deal with something you open up to a wealth of creative thinking.

Time to ask:

How would **nature deal** with the **top three challenges** in your life right now?

More creative Flip Its

If you're not a fan of nature's natural solutions then perhaps you could force some Flip It creativity. Here are three of my favourite ways to inspire creative thinking.

1 **Change the name**: Is it still the same? By changing the name of something we change how we feel about it. When you think about the word 'cup' an image comes to mind. Now think: vessel, container or chalice. What happens?

2 **Mix it up**: Who says it has to be this way? By following the same old process we tend to get the same old result. *New Thinking = New Results* – by mixing up order, numbers and processes you're sure to get new results. Start by beginning at the end and move to the beginning.

3   **Make a metaphor**: It's like ... Being able to convince people of a concept or idea is a great skill. Rather than going into great detail Flip It suggests you link your idea with a 'known' and create a metaphor. Metaphors breed metaphors, making ideas come alive.

To explain the way his company was going to change in the coming months, Stephen took a giant jigsaw puzzle to his organisation's annual conference. As he took to the stage, with jigsaw in hand and no PowerPoint support, he went on to explain that the next three months would be like building a jigsaw. They would start by finding the four corners, which he likened to the four values of the company.

Next he explained how important it was that the edges were completed. He linked this to the management of the company. Fitting the remaining pieces together, he wove in the removal of 'silo thinking' and promoted the ideals of working together, explaining that he appreciated everyone was different but that each had a place in the organisation.

Finally he shared the vision. This was what they were all working towards and, as he turned over the box lid, there was the company vision emblazoned across it.

His use of the giant jigsaw pieces as a metaphor was creative and memorable but, most importantly, throughout the day, as every speaker who followed made reference to the jigsaw, it continued to touch all of the people in the room.

Now that's a mega metaphor!

Are you feeling more creative now? What, you want more? OK, let's take Flip It for creativity to an advanced level.

I must point out the following Flip Its are not for the faint-hearted. Some, or all, of the ideas that follow could cause a mind flip of epic proportions – are you ready?

Advanced Flip It for creativity
Make it massive!

A friend of mine was in a band. They'd booked a 100-seat venue for a show and were struggling to sell tickets. He said, 'It's typical of us, we only ever sell half the tickets.' I asked him what he would do if he'd booked a venue for 1,000, 'Oh it would be a nightmare, we'd only sell half the tickets'.

I was embarrassed for him! Later that same day I encouraged him to Flip It and make it massive. I asked him to imagine he was promoting an event for 1,000 and to think about what actions he would take to sell tickets for it. He came up with five ideas in as many minutes to promote the gig.

A few weeks later, after his gig had completely sold out, he cheekily joked to me that maybe they 'should have booked a 1,000 seater'.

Link words

I love this method as an idea generator and a way to really get the creative juices flowing. The principle is very simple. Usually words are put together in certain ways which we expect. That's how they make sense. When you Flip It and mix them around, interesting things happen.

Pick a word – any word. Write this in the middle of a piece of paper. For this example I'll take the next word I hear on the radio. OK it's 'capital'.

Capital

Now add four words that are linked to capital and write them at the four corners surrounding the word capital. It doesn't matter how tenuous the links are – often that's better. I've come up with:

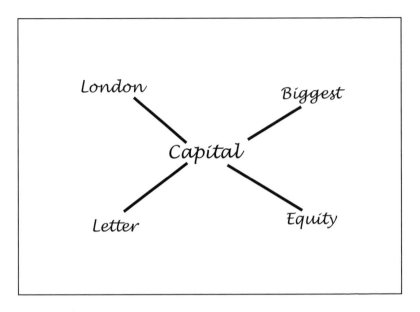

Now do the same again for each of the four words. And that's your grid.

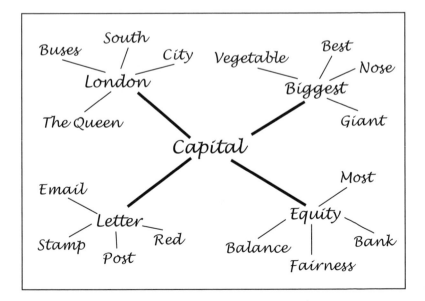

Now choose a couple of words at random and link them. What happens? Probably one of three things.

1   The two words mean nothing and don't inspire any creative thinking.

2   The two words kind of go together, you explore them, get a few ideas but nothing brilliant.

3   The two words go together and in doing so open your creativity. You think of the most amazing ideas, save the world and win a Nobel Prize.

Or it could be a combination of all three.

The secret is to test this out!

So let's do it. I'm going to capture my thoughts as I do a few *link word* combinations.

Post and *Vegetable*	Is there a need for mail-order veg? Or veg seeds. Could it be useful for very unusual vegetables? What if it was linked to a celebrity chef so you are sent the vegetables on the same day as they are presenting a TV programme so you can cook along?
Giant and *Buses*	How can we make buses bigger? What about a huge flying bus? Actually I think someone has thought of that one!
Balance and *South*	Nothing comes to mind.
Best and *Letter*	Is it best to send a letter? Should I send a letter to my best clients or best friends? What was in the best letter I ever sent or received?
Most and *Email* and *Letter*	Most communication is by email. Would it be more personal to send a letter?

Queen and *Nose* What if the Queen 'knows' something we don't? Can we ask the Queen? Could this be an idea for a book? '100 questions to ask the Queen'.

In less than five minutes I've gone from a random word I heard on the radio to a crazy idea for a book, a shift in my thinking on sending emails and a mail-order business idea.

What I like most about this method of creative idea generating is you can do it in groups or by yourself. You can grow the grid. It doesn't matter where you start, it never fails to raise a smile, plus a couple of ideas and, best of all, it's free!

Flip It for creativity is the ultimate use of Flip It thinking. My concern with most methods for improving creativity is the lack of challenges to use what you have learned. To really get the most out of Flip It for creativity you must use the tools and techniques in real-life situations.

Yes, you'll get it wrong. Yes, you'll get frustrated. And yes, you'll end up attempting to explain your brilliant ideas to others who just don't get it. However, there will be many other times when you'll get it right, you'll feel liberated and others will see you as the genius you are.

Test it at home, in your hobbies, with relationships, at work, you'll soon see.

Speaking of work, you'll probably spend a third of your life doing your job. Take off sleep and that leaves you with half your waking hours. Do you love it? Do you jump out of bed on a Monday morning shouting, 'Whoopee – it's work!'? It's a huge part of what you do, which is why you'll need to know how to ...

8

Flip It at work and in business

This chapter is going to cover all things work- and business-related: from finding the perfect job, getting the best out of the job you do, rapid promotion and even dealing with losing a job. I'm also going to cover retailing, flipping downturns, specialising and customer service – it's all here.

Even if you don't work or you're not involved with a commercial business there are dozens of Flip It tools and techniques where you can 'think transferable' and move this into other areas of life.

Why do you go to work?

Tick all of the following that apply to you.

I work:

1 just for the money ☐
2 to meet my friends ☐
3 because it's expected of me ☐
4 to make a difference ☐
5 because I have to ☐
6 because I love my job ☐
7 so that one day I don't have to ☐
8 to learn more ☐
9 all night, I work all day, to pay the bills
   I have to pay. Ain't it sad? ☐

If you ticked mainly odd numbers then I guess work is a bit of a 'means to an end' for you. You don't love it, but you have to do it.

If you ticked mainly even numbers then you love work so much that you'd probably do it for free!

And if you ticked just 9 then you've been listening to far too much Abba!

The first part of this chapter is about: using **Flip It** so you

love your job *and* you get paid well for **doing it**.

How to get paid for what you love to do

The foundation for this is to go back to basics. Take a look at your list of why you go to work. Did you tick number 4 – 'I go to work to make a difference'? I believe this is the number one reason to get out of bed and clock in.

I regularly work with teachers and lecturers in schools and colleges. As they arrive, many have a touch of cynicism and morale can be low. My job is to get them to feel motivated and excited about the work they do.

In my view teachers have one of the most important jobs in the world and with that in mind I'll ask them what they think *they really do*. When I suggest that they are *directly involved with improving the quality of life of often some of the most vulnerable people in our society* some may sneer, but most quite visibly have a mental flash to the very reason why they wanted to work in education – to make a difference.

And that's the challenge.

Sometimes it is so **obvious** we **miss it**.

Here's how you can change your thinking using Flip It for your work.

The 'What do I really do?' Flip It

Just take a moment to answer these three questions about what *you really do*.

1 Who benefits from what you do?
2 How does this make them feel?
3 How does this make you feel?

Once, while I was teaching these three simple questions a despondent participant called Claire said, 'This doesn't apply to me because I just work in a shop.'

After a little investigation I discovered she worked in a clothes shop, which I thought was brilliant. It took a little while for her to get her head around this concept but here's how the exchange went.

•Brilliant, you work in a clothes shop. So what do you do there Claire?•

•Sell clothes.•

•And what is the most common question people ask when they approach you in the shop?•

•It's normally something about size or price.•

•Great! Then what do you do?•

•Tell them the price or find them the size.•

I take a deep breath and realise I need to dig a bit deeper so I ask: •Do you ever offer advice when you answer those questions?•

•Well, if we don't have the size or something costs too much then I'll show them something else.•

•And are people happy with that, Claire?•

•Of course. Most times people haven't got a clue what they really need anyway.•

•And you help them with that choice?•

•Yes, I think so.•

•And how do people feel when you've given them good advice?•

•Oh, they love it!•

•And how does that make you feel?•

•Oh that's ace. It's the best bit of the job.•

Bingo! She got it. Claire makes people feel good by helping them to look good. That is a cool job! Now that Claire goes to work with that thought foremost in her mind she's having a much better time.

Flip Bit

Work takes on new meaning when you link what you do with helping people improve their lives. Focus on these aspects and you're on your way to making work wonderful every day.

I'm sure you know what I'm going to ask you to do next. Use the simple, 'What Do I Really Do?' Flip It tool and ask the three questions about your work. If you're happy with your answers, then focus on keeping those thoughts foremost in your mind during every working day. It's not the solution to every work worry but it is a good foundation to build on.

Now let's get specific and explore some other areas of working life and business where you can apply Flip It thinking for the best possible results.

Using Flip It to find the perfect job

What if you don't have a job or you are looking for a new one? Would you like to know how to land the perfect post?

Have you ever applied for a job and been unsuccessful? Most of us know that feeling, but I wonder how many of us take the time to ask, 'If 20 people applied but only 1 was successful, what did "the 1" have that the rest of us didn't?'

An unemployed friend of mine recently told me he was applying for 10 jobs a day online and had been doing this for 3 months with no luck. How long would it take for you to realise that that particular strategy wasn't really working?

If you're aiming to get the job of your dreams and not getting there, then perhaps your current strategy could do with a shake-up.

Flip It thinkers are doing something you're not – that's why they get the best jobs. Here's a taste of what they do.

1 **Stay in work – even if you hate it:** Flip It thinkers have in mind the perfect job they want but, in the meantime, they do anything to remain employed. Employers are happier employing people who are already in a job. They would rather employ someone who was doing a job that is completely different from the job they have applied for than employ someone who isn't working.

2 **Take all the risk:** Imagine saying to a prospective employer, 'I will work for free for you for the first month. Then pay me just 50 per cent of the advertised wage for the second month and only after those two months, if I have proven to you that I am worth 100 per cent of the salary you are offering, will you need to pay me at the full rate.' OK, not everyone can afford to do this, but for a dream job could you find a way?

3 **Do your homework:** Most people apply for jobs and turn up at interviews with little or no knowledge about the organisation they want to work for. Flip It and turn up with an arsenal of knowledge about your new organisation

4 **Get out there:** Sending 20 copies of your CV off and waiting to hear back is no longer (and I doubt ever was) a very effective way of job hunting. You need to be building your networks, getting out there and meeting the right people and letting them know about you and your skills. Making sure that you are the first to know about new opportunities. Then you can be the one choosing who you want to work for. Yes, I did say choosing.

Here's what Martin Beeson did when his company announced they were moving the marketing department to America and he was being made redundant. He wrote a letter of introduction and attached it to his CV. He took 20 copies and attended a local net-working meeting where most people were entrepreneurs trying to sell products and services. He was there selling a very important product – himself. He worked the room and gave his CV, letter and a brief introduction about what he was doing to 20 people. Just 24 hours later he'd had 3 job offers.

Martin now lives and works on the West Coast of Australia working as a marketing manager for a company who make and sell luxury boats. You don't achieve that by sitting at home applying for jobs online.

5 **Make yourself magnificent:** When you do get a chance to be face to face with a decision maker make sure you shine. I've interviewed hundreds of people for jobs large and small. Some, who really believed they were doing a good job in the interview, were so bad I wouldn't let them look after my cat. Yet others have had me thinking, 'I hope they will want to work for me' and I've sold them the job!

If you don't get a job, it's worth asking for a bit of 'honest Joe feedback'. This means you ask for feedback warts and all. It can sting a bit but, if you get the same message more than twice, you know you need to change.

6 **Extra mile everything:** Check your spelling, grammar and facts (twice). Use good paper (minimum 100 gsm) and send documents via registered post. When you get an interview do a travel dry run so you know where you're going, turn up early and look professional. Floss your teeth, check your breath, check your shoes, check everything!

These are the things that most people don't even know they should do. Or worse still know they should be doing them but just don't!

My advice? Don't be most people.

Rapid promotion

The people who get rapid promotion aren't thinking in the same way as those who trudge up the corporate ladder. Fortunately for you, most people believe that the best way to get promoted is to be a corporate crawler, a direct member of the boss' family or just plain lucky.

The truth is far from that. In fact most people who

get promoted (especially those who are promoted rapidly) have one thing in common: they add more value to the bottom line than the others. Or, if you work for a 'not for profit' organisation, they add more to the mission-critical results.

Have you ever heard the expression 'success leaves tracks'? In simple terms, people who are successful can't help but leave the template of how they did it behind them and that's good news for you.

Here's how Flip It thinkers can use this knowledge to get promoted quickly.

Old thinking	New thinking
They must have been sucking up to the boss to get promoted	I wonder what they did to get promoted? I'll find out
When they pay me more I'll do more	I'll do more now and get paid more later
They're just lucky	What's their strategy and how can I use it?
It's not what you know, it's who you know	Who do I need to know? How can I meet them?

Flip It on a really bad day – what to do if you lose your job

I sincerely hope you never have to use the techniques in this section but, if you should find yourself in a situation where you have lost your job, then here are a few ideas which I'm sure will help.

It's not your fault: You worked hard. You gave 100 per cent commitment then one day, wham, you've lost your livelihood. When others feel despondent and pessimistic could you Flip It and feel hopeful and positive? It's a tough choice but to make it easier here are some Flip It tools.

Park the resentment: It's easier said than done, but leave the resentment for another day. Or if you do need to get it out of your system, then do it quickly (five minutes) and quietly. We all know what the boss is and where he can stick his Bentley so why not Flip It and be different?

The most important action now is to think about you and what you are going to do next.

Don't take it personally: So why did you have to go when Doreen in Accounts, who everyone knows is next to useless, got to stay? Questions like this will wear you down, create a wedge of doubt (see page 129) over your ability and ultimately hold you back. The chances are you didn't do anything wrong other than being in the wrong post at the wrong time. Now what can you do ...

Be a first mover: I grew up in a town called Consett, County Durham. In 1980 the local steelworks closed with the loss of 3,700 jobs. I remember at the time, when people were given their redundancy payments, hearing former steel workers saying they were 'going to take a couple of months off and then look for work'.

What actually happened was, after they had taken the couple of months off they found: (a) it was very difficult to motivate themselves to find a new job; (b) the jobs that had been available at time of closure were gone; (c) it was going to take several months or even years before the money available for new economic growth was going to create enough new jobs to go around.

Meanwhile another group had used Flip It thinking and taken what I call a 'first mover advantage'. As soon as they knew their fate they quickly started the process of finding a new job.

Grasp your facts: Capture on paper as much knowledge as you can which may be helpful to you later. A short pencil is better than a long memory! By writing down names and numbers of contacts, specific knowledge you have and your ways of working you could be capturing valuable information to help you in the future.

Be careful who you spend your time with: You become like the people who you spend most of your time with. So although it may be tempting to spend time with other people who are unemployed, Flip It and don't. Spend as much of your time as you can with people who are in employment. You will get a job faster by doing this.

Complete a skills audit: Many of these can be found online and they consist of a list of attributes you may have. They usually ask you to tick a box or score yourself out of 10. Rather than simply printing and completing the audit add three extra words and a brief description after you tick a box. The three words are: 'which means that'.

Here's how this may work with some skills audit questions.

I am able to work to deadlines *which means that I can organise my time, increase reliability and don't create unnecessary worry.*

I am practical *which means that I can fix things, rather than calling for help. I am able to use this skill to help others.*

I have good use of grammar *which means that I can proofread documents prepared for others, improving the professionalism of an organisation.*

Most people think of their skills as a list. The real value in any skill is the benefit it brings to others.

By adding the 'which means that' statement and extending the skill, you increase your value, self-worth and employability.

Look after yourself: Losing your job can be a very stressful experience. *You* are the most important person in the world so it's more important than ever that you stay (or get) fit, eat well and find time to relax properly (which doesn't mean watching daytime TV).

Is it time to work for you?

Is it time to Flip It and be your own boss? Many entrepreneurs started their businesses because they lost their job. It turned out that their redundancy was a blessing in disguise.

Being an entrepreneur doesn't necessarily mean you have to start a big company, employ lots of staff and take masses of risks. It could be that you become self-employed doing something that you've always loved. Losing your job could be the opportunity you've been waiting for.

It's worth taking a few minutes to review this chapter so far and make sure you have at least a couple of the ideas ready to take action on. Work is such a huge area of your time it should also be one of the most enjoyable and rewarding parts of your life. When you use Flip It at work you'll soon see how getting the best out of your job is easier than you think.

Flip Bit

For many people over half of their waking hours are spent getting to work, working then travelling home. Which means that ... you'd better enjoy what you do!

Flip It in business

Perhaps you feel inspired to start your own organisation, to step up and create something new. Or do you want to make your organisation better? If so you'll need to understand how important it is to Flip It in business.

If you're 'in business' – and for the purpose of this book let's make that anyone who owns a business, leads in a business or feels they have a responsibility for the success of the business they work for – then this section is for you.

Buying art in Paris – how to use the extras to make money

Parisian street artists make a great deal of their money from the little extras they sell. Here's how they do it.

When you buy a picture, a caricature or sketch you will rarely see the artist displaying a price. When you ask them the price they may say, '50 euros'. Then they will watch your reaction very carefully. If you flinch they will then add some additional value by completing their sentence with something like, '... but today I am also offering a free frame worth 10 euros' ... and if you are still flinching they'll add ... 'and a nice box to keep it safe for the journey home, which would normally cost another 10 euros'.

It's a deal. Think about it, you got €70 worth of stuff for just €50. Clever you! Now what happens when they find someone who is happy with the €50 asking price?

Just at the point of transaction when you are happy with the €50 price they will say, 'How would you like me to add a nice frame? It's only 10 euros?' The happy tourist keeps smiling and nodding as the artist adds, '... and how about a nice box to keep it safe for the journey home, it's only another 10 euros?'

This is brilliant Flip It thinking which can be used during any transaction. Try it when you are buying. If you can't negotiate a reduction, ask for something in addition to the item you are interested in. Try it when you are selling. If the price seems too much for your customer, what can you add without discounting your price? If they jump at the price, what else can you add while your customer is in a buying mood?

Specialise

Smyth & Gibson make the best shirts in the world. The Belfast-based shirt makers focus on making shirts, shirts and nothing but shirts. They offer a 20-year guarantee – on a shirt!

But it gets better than that. Smyth & Gibson employ staff who just make and attach collars to shirts. That's all they do – world-class collar attachers. They employ people who just cut cloth in a way that makes every seam appear seamless. They employ people who just attach sleeves and match stripes perfectly. In fact 15 people are involved with each and every shirt.

'So why not teach people to do a little bit of everything? Surely you'd make more shirts?' I asked Richard Gibson. He told me how his Flip It thinking was transforming the way they made shirts. Where everyone else was automating and looking for volume they were specialising and focusing on detail. I challenged him and asked, 'Why is it so important to match the stripes, as most people wouldn't even notice you've done it?' He simply replied, 'We notice.'

I love that confidence and certainty.

> **Flip Bit**
>
> In a world of generalists, what do you do best?

Flip It by using negatives

In the 1970s Allen, Brady and Marsh (ABM) were an exciting brash advertising agency. They were lucky enough to be on the final list to pitch for the British Rail account. At that time, British Rail was one of the biggest accounts in the country and highly prized. So how do you go about winning an account like that?

Several agencies on the shortlist decided to 'woo' the chairman and the board with fancy slogans, mocked-up adverts and slick presentations.

ABM decided to Flip It.

A disinterested receptionist greeted the British Rail chairman and his board before taking them to a dingy meeting room. Although there were seven of them, there were chairs for only six. Lukewarm tea, soggy biscuits and curly-edged sandwiches were served and, worse still, the team from ABM was late.

After an excruciating hour, and with the chairman about to leave, the head of ABM, Rod Allen, walked into the room. He didn't apologise and barely acknowledged the BR chairman. To say the British Rail representatives were livid was an understatement.

Then one of the best pieces of Flip It thinking to win an account was revealed. Rod Allen simply gestured around the room and said, 'This is what your customers think of you, and we're going to change it.'

They got the account.

Oh weren't they the lucky ones? How many times have you heard the word 'lucky' used when someone has a major success? The truth is often far from that.

In most cases this **so-called 'luck'** is where individuals have brought together **imagination, foresight, acumen** and a good dose of graft to create something **different and memorable**.

Flip Bit

Flip It thinking in business gets you recommended, remembered and referred.

Turning a downturn into an opportunity

Business has good times and bad times. When things are going well it's hard to imagine that things can go wrong. But they will. When things are going badly it's hard to imagine how they will pick up. But they will. Smart people know this and very smart people know how to profit from it.

A mate of mine sold 38 properties in 2 months because he couldn't believe how much money he was making on them. He did this about 2 months before the 2007 housing stall and obviously well before the 2008 housing crash. How did he know?

You may think he was lucky but in fact he was just very intuitive. When you ask him how he knew, he always replies, 'It just felt too good to be true.' Many other people who invested in property were caught out because not only did it feel too good to be true – it was.

Knowing that cycles occur like this it's tempting to wait for an upturn before putting in effort, starting new projects or taking a risk. However, the very smart don't think like that, they Flip It, double their efforts, start extra projects and take more risks. They know that when the good times re-emerge they'll be at the forefront and they'll reap the rewards.

The downturn Flip It

Here are four questions to ask in a downturn.

1 What do we do best?
2 How can we diversify or specialise now?
3 How can we create more customer loyalty?
4 What can we do now to maximise our business once the upturn comes?

The good times Flip It

And here are some more for when the going is good.

1 Are we investing for the future?
2 WHow can we further flex and diversify our risk muscle?
3 Where else in the world can we do what we do?
4 Is this too good to be true?

I don't know what times you are experiencing as you read *Flip It* but I do know that the opposite will be the case at some point in the future. My challenge to you is to use as many Flip It tools as you can to maximise your business now and reap the rewards in the future.

If you'd like a further wake-up call on this read *The Great Crash, 1929*, by John Kenneth Galbraith (Penguin, 1992).

Think like a customer

Who and what else could you think like to Flip It and get different results? You'll frequently hear people saying during important inter-departmental meetings that we must 'think like a customer'. Nice, but what does that really mean?

The best way to think like a customer is to be a customer.

I worked with a company (who will remain nameless for this example) who were concerned that their online sales business wasn't being used as much as they had hoped. I was working with their senior directors and asked, 'How many of you have ever ordered something from your own company online?'

Almost everyone nodded. Then I took a file from my case and continued with, 'I have a list of all the people who have ordered online and I've had it cross-referenced with the participants here. Please raise your hand if you know for certain that you are on this list because you have made an online order. Only a few hands went up. Ten faces went very red, including a now purple chief executive.

How could they truly begin to think like their customers when they had no experience of their own online offering?

Flip Bit

You have to test it by doing it, living it and breathing it.

A brilliant example of really thinking like a customer comes from the Summer Lodge Hotel in Dorset. Julia was getting married on 2 January and in preparation had had 'gel' nails applied on New Year's Eve. Unfortunately, 24 hours later (New Year's Day), 3 had fallen off and she wasn't too sure how much she liked the ones remaining. Unfortunately, the salon she had visited for her manicure had closed. Her wedding was the very next day and she was in a panic.

She called Summer Lodge and talked to the Spa manager, Rosemary Sumner-Pike, and begged her to help. An appointment was made for her later that same day (again this is New Year's Day, when many places are closed). Here's where Rosemary did some brilliant Flip It thinking. She gathered her team and got them to imagine that it was the day before their wedding and asked them to consider how they felt and what it would take to make this a very special visit.

On her arrival Julia was given camomile tea to help her stay calm. The old nails were removed and a manicure carried out. Then the big decision: what colour should her nails be painted? She couldn't decide between bright red and pale pink. So the manicurist painted her nails on one hand red, and the other pale pink.

Unfortunately she still couldn't decide as she commented that her make-up wasn't done and her hair was down.

Here's where the Summer Lodge Spa stepped up to super service. As one member of staff applied her make-up another put her hair up whist a third made another cup of camomile tea. With the look complete the decision was made: bright red!

As Julia left she promised to stay in touch. Little did they know how soon this would be.

Her wedding went beautifully, the reception was magical but, when Julia and her new husband arrived at 11 pm outside the hotel they had chosen for their wedding night, they were amazed to find it was closed. Here's where all that thinking like a customer started to pay off. Who did the newlyweds decide to call? Yup, Summer Lodge. They booked the best room, stayed for most of the next day, enjoyed lunch and had further treatments in the Spa.

We've all heard this type of story before; maybe something similar has happened to you. What makes these situations magical is the human element. If Rosemary hadn't encouraged her staff to really 'think like a customer', do you think they would have created such magic? Do you think Julia and her new husband would have turned to Summer Lodge when their original accommodation plans went wrong?

How likely are they to **tell anyone** who will listen about their **five star experience**?

Flip It for small retailers (and how the big boys can do this too)

I'm often amazed when smaller businesses think the secret of success is to be more like the big ones, when in fact the opposite is true.

In my local town we had only two fishmongers, and life was good for the fishy folk. Then within two years we were bestowed with a Tesco, Waitrose and Marks & Spencer. I love buying fresh fish, so keenly observed what happened next to my local *purveyors of poissons*.

Fishmonger one started to complain about Tesco. He complained to the local press, the other retailers and even his customers. I remember him telling me that he couldn't compete on price with Tesco (I hadn't even asked about price!) After a lame and bitter fight he closed and even put a notice in his window blaming Tesco et al.

Fishmonger two was different. She got to work creating a local brand and local loyalty. She would tell you about the fish, when and where it was caught and offer some little extras if you spent a few pounds more. She must have felt the effects of the three new arrivals in town but she didn't complain once. She survived, thrived and, since her rival closed, she's never been busier.

Flip Bit

Don't try to be like the big boys. Find out what they don't do that you can and what you do that they can't.

And if you are a **big retailer**, what can you learn from the **smaller guys**?
Warmth? Pace? Individualism?

When you're the big guy it's worthwhile taking the opportunity to Flip It and learn from those who are smaller (and better?) than you.

The world of 'business' big and small needs to Flip It now more than ever. Ideas, pace and enthusiasm are more important than ever. So is a clear vision of where you want to be. That's why you must …

9

Flip It for your fantastic future

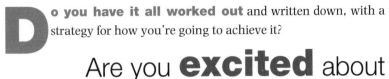

Do you have it all worked out and written down, with a strategy for how you're going to achieve it?

Are you **excited** about your **future**? Or are you **wondering** what you'll be doing this time **next week**?

Is creating a fantastic future as simple as writing down a few goals? It's an easy first step and we all know we should do this but there's actually a whole lot more to creating a fantastic future.

One of my observations as I travel and meet people, is how many don't have a plan for their future. Most simply allow life to happen to them. Then they use their energy to deal with the results. I say Flip It, plan the life you want and use your energy and creativity to make it happen.

Many people set unnecessary personal conditions on the planning of their futures and in doing so they actually never get started. I call them the 'if ... then' thinkers.

The danger of 'if ... then'

'If ... then' thinking is undoubtedly one of the most disempowering ways to think. You've heard people say it a thousand times: 'If I made more money, then I would save'; 'If my boss gave me a promotion, then I'd work harder'; 'If I had a new car, then I'd keep it clean'.

When you think this way, you place your future in the hands of circumstances over which you have little or no control.

It's a **challenging** cycle to break, but **break it** you must.

People also use 'if ... then' thinking when it comes to their personal happiness: 'If I weighed less, then I'd be happy'; 'If I had the right person in my life, then things would be different', etc.

Here's a thought. Do you think if you were to Flip It you might get better results? What if you had an attitude of, 'I'm happy therefore I find it easier to manage my weight.' Or 'By being happy I'm attracting the right person into my life.' Sounds simple but just wanting to be happy is not enough, you have to make happy happen.

Once you have the realisation that you and you alone are in control of your actions, attitudes and beliefs, then you have the perfect platform on which to build your fantastic future.

There are times when you can use a bit of 'if ... then' thinking in a positive way to motive yourself. How about this?

If you want to create a **fantastic future**, then you'd better start working on it **right now**.

'Is it time to write my goals down now?' you ask. No, not yet (but I love your enthusiasm). We haven't explored exactly what you want your future to look like yet – but I'm sure you agree that you want it to be fantastic.

With which of these statements do you concur?

1 I deserve a fantastic future.
2 The actions I take today will impact on my future.
3 I have choice over the majority of my actions.
4 In the past I have overcome obstacles to get to where I am today.
5 I know deep down that I'm better than I think.

I'm guessing that on paper you will have agreed with all of them. And why not – they are all true.

Now let's take those five simple statements and look at some of the ways people subconsciously (or even consciously) sabotage them.

1   I deserve a fantastic future.

Only lucky people end up with a fantastic future. I'm very average.

2   The actions I take today will impact on my future.

Therefore I can put them off until tomorrow or next week, it won't make that much difference.

3   I have choice over the majority of my actions.

Other than the big ones, which all seem to be made for me by my boss, the bank, the weather, etc.

4   In the past I have overcome obstacles to get to where I am today.

Because they are in the past I don't remember how I felt about the obstacle or the joy of overcoming it. My mind is currently focused on the size of the ones ahead.

5   I know deep down that I'm better than I think.

But I find it easier to beat myself up over what I'm not very good at and become very modest about my skills.

The trick here is to recognise that you have a choice over the way you choose to perceive these situations.

Sometimes the **more positive** proactive choice takes a little more **effort, self-confidence and belief** but the results make going for it **worth it**.

The realm of opportunity and the wedge of doubt

Your first challenge is to learn how to focus your mind to the 'realm of opportunity' and in doing so eliminate the 'wedge of doubt'. And yes, I still haven't asked you to write down what you want for the future – yet.

The realm of opportunity

So what is the realm of opportunity? I believe it's a deep knowing that, in time, with the right attitude, action and dedication, anyone can achieve great things.

How long do you think it takes to become one of the world's top five sommeliers? About 20, 30, 40 years? Actually it's four.

That's how many years it took Luvo Ntezo of the Twelve Apostles Hotel in South Africa, to progress from a pool porter to one of the world's best sommeliers. This is his story.

'The first time someone ordered a bottle of wine from me, it was a disaster. I couldn't even work the opener and a guest had to help me. I decided there and then to learn more about wine.' That was the moment when Luvo began his journey in the study of wine.

When Luvo was offered an opportunity to visit the wine cellar of his hotel he jumped at the chance. While he was there he met winemaker John Laubscher and cellar master Herman Hanekom.

'I asked ridiculous questions, and those two wonderful men answered them all', he says.

As time went on he developed a great 'nose' but a mentor of his explained to Luvo that he 'lacked the poetic language of wine'.

'I worked hard on improving my English by reading', says Luvo, who would often study for hours a day alongside his job. Soon after, he was offered a job as a barman at the Twelve Apostles Leopard Lounge.

Even though he had begun in a junior position, he quickly made his mark at a wine-tasting event. A bottle of wine was opened and tasted; everyone nodded and said, 'it was nice'. However, when Luvo tasted it he thought it was horrible and said so. 'Oxidised, flat and dull', was his honest opinion – and he was right.

The management at the Twelve Apostles were intrigued and Luvo was offered the opportunity to perfect his craft.

A couple of years later he went on to win first place in the Young Sommeliers category of the national Chaîne des Rôtisseurs competition, and qualified to compete in the international contest in Vienna where he came fourth. Amazing too when you consider Luvo achieved this at just 25 years old.

Let's break it down and take a look at how Luvo achieved this remarkable goal in just four years and how he used his version of Flip It to make it happen.

- **Step 1   He used a problem as a motivator:** He was embarrassed that he didn't know how to open a bottle of wine and made a decision to Flip It and 'learn more about wine'.

    I wonder how many people think like that. Maybe most would figure out what they could do to avoid serving wine after such an embarrassing situation.

- **Step 2   He asked 'ridiculous questions':** I love this part of his story for two reasons. One, he asked them. How many ridiculous questions remain unanswered in your head because you are too embarrassed to ask?

    Second, he credits the 'wonderful men who answered them'. Wonderful people who will answer your ridiculous questions are everywhere. People like Luvo who will ask them aren't.

- **Step 3   He worked hard at his craft:** Developing a great 'nose' for wine isn't down to luck, it's down to effort. Before the final competition, Luvo spent weeks tasting hundreds of wines, learning their history and preparing himself for every eventuality.

- **Step 4 He took criticism on the chin and did something about it:** How would you have felt if you were doing really well with your skill and someone suggested your use of language wasn't up to scratch? Once again, Luvo took a negative and chose to Flip It into a positive, spending much of his spare time studying English and developing his use of the language.

- **Step 5 He took a risk:** At the wine tasting, when everyone acted like sheep saying the wine was 'nice', Luvo chose to Flip It and followed his heart. Can you imagine the pressure of being the new boy at your first tasting and suggesting the 'expert' had got it wrong?

- **Step 6 He had a nurturing, supportive environment:** He was surrounded by people who wanted to support him to achieve his goal. I'm sure this accelerated his journey to success.

- **Step 7 He was prepared to be tested:** By entering a competition and having people you don't know judge you, you are taking a huge risk. But with risk comes reward.

There are dozens of stories like Luvo's and I spend much of my time reading and being inspired by them. Luvo's story is a perfect example of embracing the realm of opportunity. But what about its cousin, the wedge of doubt?

The wedge of doubt

This is what stops people from progressing or even getting started: 'Why should I bother to set goals for a fantastic future, I'll never succeed'. As we weren't born with that belief you have to wonder where this thinking starts.

I worked with a teacher at a school in Glasgow, presenting a goal-setting workshop to her class. One of the girls decided she wanted to be an air hostess (or flight cabin attendant, nowadays). She created a fantastic goal sheet which included a strong affirmation and a picture of her wearing the uniform. She was feeling excited and motivated.

Her teacher looked over her work and I was gobsmacked when she said, 'That goal is very nice, but I think you should have something a little more realistic to fall back on.'

Wham! The wedge of doubt was in place and I was speechless. After the lesson I challenged the teacher on her thinking and was even more aghast when she said, 'It's all very good having goals but what if she ends up being disappointed?'

Wouldn't you just love to show that teacher how wrong she was at 35,000 feet?

Flip Bit

Don't allow any room for the wedge of doubt. Use other people's negative comments and opinions to motivate you. Be determined to succeed. The only person who should decide how far you can go is you!

Are you starting to feel motivated now? Yes! And I still haven't suggested you write your goals down.

As well as being concerned by the number of people who don't have a future plan, I am equally surprised by the number of people who, plan or no plan, haven't actually decided what it is they want.

It's pretty **hard to achieve** a **fantastic future** if you don't know **what you want**.

Perhaps the following list might help to get your future planning juices flowing.

The Flip It idea generator

Maintain vibrant health	Buy a new car	Move to a nicer house
Pay off your debts	Learn a language	Plan a weekend away
Be a few pounds lighter	Find a partner	Experience the trip of a lifetime
Write a book	Learn how to cook	Run a marathon (or half one)
Landscape your garden	Buy a new outfit	Spend more time with friends
Build an extension	Get a new job	Start your own business
Give more to charity	Go on a road trip	Have more 'me time'
Learn how to surf	Quit smoking	Take salsa lessons
Pay off your mortgage	Retire early	Have masses of energy
Sign up for a course	Read more	Know what you want to do next
Get organised	Water ski	Build self-confidence
Sleep under the stars	Simplify life	Eat in the best restaurants
Go on a cruise	Volunteer	Live in the country

So, 39 suggestions to kick-start your imagination. I could write thousands but that would end up being *my* list. It's time to write yours – *yes it's time now* – but you're going to do it Flip It style.

Goals and the cost of 'not'

Normally when you are encouraged to write an initial list of goals, it's followed by a session where you describe the benefits of achieving that goal. As you're going to Flip It, I'd like you to write one line about what will happen if you *don't* achieve that goal.

Here are some examples.

Pay off my mortgage	If I don't I will always be tied to my lender and never know how it feels to fully own my home.
Read more	I know reading makes me better so just imagine what I may miss out on if I don't.
Quit smoking	If I don't I'm likely to die a horrible, painful death which will affect every one of my friends and family.

Ouch!

By creating a **negative consequence** you also create leverage to **get you started** on your goal.

Flip Bit

You will probably do more to avoid pain than you will to gain pleasure.

Once you have used this method to kick-start you into action you can rewrite your list with the positive descriptions of how your future will look when you have achieved these goals. Using the power of pain avoidance is a great way to get started but don't hold on to it for the long term.

Your future can be as short term as a few weeks or as long term as decades, but it's important you consider when you want your goals to be achieved. After all a goal is just a dream unless you put a date on it.

And while I'm stating the obvious, just setting the goal isn't enough – you have to do something, take action, get busy, make it happen!

So let's make a few assumptions so you can take Flip It for a fantastic future to the next stage.

So far you have:

- decided what you want;
- written it down (put a date on when each goal will be achieved)
- thought about what will happen if you don't achieve your goals to get you motivated;
- taken action to move towards your goals;
- rewritten your list with positive descriptions;
- followed the basic rules of goal-setting, by reviewing your goals regularly and visualising yourself achieving them.

All done? Good work! What next?

Overcoming obstacles

Wouldn't life be peachy if we had no obstacles or problems to overcome? Well, actually no, it would be dull, dull, dull.

Your ability to overcome obstacles is the single biggest factor in how quickly and successfully you will achieve your goals for a fantastic future. The bigger the goal the bigger the obstacles.

Flip It thinkers love obstacles because, once they have been tackled, your knowledge and experience have grown and you have always moved closer to your goal. In the Flip It for success chapter of this book on page 80 I share a tool called 'Rock to resolution'. This tool offers a simple way to turn problems into solutions. Once you have a basic understanding of this model it makes it easier to understand that problems are a gift.

You may have heard of a chap called Sir Isaac Newton who's third law said (more or less), 'For every action there is always an opposite and equal reaction.' Well, here is Heppell's first Flip It Law:

For every **negative** there is a much more **powerful positive** just waiting to **blow it away**.

Flip Bit

Problems are good – the bigger the better. Bring them on!

By coming to terms with this you free up your thinking, accept challenges and become more aware of the many positive solutions available.

There are countless examples of people who have embraced this thinking to achieve great things. Perhaps the most famous is Nelson Mandela who, after 27 years in prison, used his time, experiences and great thought in a positive way to change a nation.

I wonder what you or I would be thinking after 27 years in a jail. Nelson Mandela has received over 100 awards in recognition of his work, including the Nobel Peace Prize in 1993. That's a Flip.

To Flip It for a fantastic future you have to embrace challenges and see beyond them. Often these rocks seem so large it's difficult to imagine how you'll get past them. But you will. You can choose to break through as quickly or slowly as you like. You'll choose fast, knowing that those who take massive action get massive results – every time.

Flip Bit

There is always a way.

I believe you deserve a fantastic future of success, wealth, recognition, vibrant health, opportunity, fun, love and laughter. At times that can seem far away but, if I was to tell you it's often closer than you think, might that give you the oomph you need to really go for it? And I mean *really go for it*! Brilliant time to get busy and tie up a few loose ends with ...

10

Flip It for everything else

By now you will be well-versed in the Flip It way of thinking. In fact, you could probably write some Flip It ideas of your own, and maybe you should.

This final chapter is a rapid-fire way to cover all the ideas that didn't fit naturally into the other chapters, a few totally random thoughts, some stories of how others have used Flip It and a call to action so you'll get off your backside and make things happen.

Turning what's wrong into what's right

The grateful list. This is a timeless classic which involves you using a bit of Flip It when you are having one of your 'the whole world is against me' moments. It's very easy to feel this way and indulge in a 'pity party'. When it's time to slap yourself out of it, take a pen, a piece of paper and five minutes out of your busy life and write 'All the things I'm grateful for' at the top of a page.

Now start your grateful list. Add everything you can, large and small. Here are a few ideas to get you started:

- I'm alive.
- I have food in my house.
- My family loves me.
- I can see the world.
- The rest of my life starts now.
- I can walk.
- I am free.
- I have a job.
- The best is yet to come.
- I'm healthy.
- I can smile.
- The sun shone today.
- I have free choice.
- I believe in free will.
- I have a choice of clothes.

- The ability to change is down to me.
- I can read.
- I have clean water.
- My bed is warm, dry and comfortable.

Once you have exhausted your list, take a moment to review each item. Start with the words 'I am grateful ...' add an item from your list and consider what this means in your life right now.

It's amazing how, by doing such a simple **Flip It**, you can **turn despair into hope**.

Hope is a strategy

A few years ago, I read a book called *Hope is Not a Strategy* by Rick Page (McGraw-Hill, 2003). One recent Sunday morning I decided he was wrong – hope *is* a strategy and a very good one.

I was in Leadgate Methodist Church listening to a brilliant man and one of my great mentors, Reverend Barrie Lees, talk about St Paul. He quoted Paul as saying, 'Let hope keep you joyful.' Aren't they wonderful words? 'Let hope keep you joyful.'

Barrie went on to explain the different levels of hope; from minor hope – i.e. I hope it doesn't rain or I hope I can park, to major hope – i.e. I hope they find a cure, or hope for the world.

Hope keeps people going.
Hope wins when all else may have failed.
Hope can keep you joyful.

What are you hoping for?

In the past, I might have been of the opinion that hope wasn't enough and I would have encouraged you that the only way was to take massive action if you wanted results. Today I think there's room for both.

Travelling home after the service in the car with my family, we each shared a couple of hopes: 'I hope I get an easy exam'; 'I hope I get the garden finished'; 'I hope my appraisal goes well'; 'I hope I'm being a brilliant Dad' were just some of the 'hopes' we shared.

We felt better. We were in fact joyful. Paul was right. No offence to Rick Page – his book has some great content – but I think Paul has outsold him in the bestseller lists!

Finding something you've lost

This one could be described as a bit mental and takes Flip It to a whole new level but I've found it works for me.

Have you ever lost something and found yourself in a blind panic wondering where it could have gone? I'm sure you have and I'm sure you've experienced that crazy activity where you end up looking in the same place again and again with naïve desperation that the item may magically turn up there.

I once lost a very important document and I was frantic, searching high and low. A new friend of mine suggested a crazy way to find it – so crazy you'll have to Flip your thinking if you want it to work. .

She took off her necklace and suggested I hold it over the palm of my left hand. Then I had to say, 'Show me yes, show me yes, show me yes' over and over until the chain reacted. It did and started to swing from left to right.

Next I was asked to follow the same procedure again, but this time to say, 'Show me no', repeatedly. This time the necklace swayed from front to back.

Now that I had established my 'yes' and 'no' swings it was simply a matter of elimination to find the missing document. I remember it very clearly:

Is the document in the house?	No
Is it in my office?	Yes
Is the document close to my desk?	Yes
Is it on my desk?	No
Is the document in a drawer of my desk?	Yes
Is it in the top drawer?	No
Is it in the middle drawer?	Yes
Is the document easy to see?	No
Is it in something else?	Yes

The next morning I could barely contain my excitement as I walked into the office. I gingerly opened the middle drawer, took out a pile of papers and there in the middle of a magazine was the document I had lost. It immediately came flooding back to me that I had had the document with me while on a train. I must have packed it away with the magazine in my case. Then when I emptied the case into my desk's second drawer down (a time management technique for another day) I'd put the missing document in there too.

My logical brain tells me that this is nonsense; a swinging chain can't find missing items. But when you Flip It – and become even more logical it makes perfect sense.

The swaying is caused by the tiny movements you make with your hands. The more you sway, the more it moves and the more it moves the more you sway.

My memory (brilliant and perfect as it is) remembered the document being inadvertently placed in the magazine.

Remember your **memory is perfect**; it's your recall that **could be better**.

The chain simply acted as a channel between my memory and my physical motion.

It's a whacky one but I double dare you to test it.

The A–Z of music

Graham Willis became a music knowledge superstar in the most amazing way. To really appreciate this, you have to go back to that time when you bought albums from shops.

At the age of 14 or 15, when everyone else was buying the latest release or fad band of the moment Graham decided to Flip It and do something completely different. He wanted to build an eclectic music collection and did so ... alphabetically.

So he began in the first week by buying an album by an artist whose name began with the letter 'A', the next week 'B' and so on. After just two years he had the most diverse music collection you could imagine alongside an amazingly varied taste in music and a guaranteed seat at every pop quiz.

How could you apply Graham's Flip It thinking to one of your interests?

The big clear up

Are you a hoarder? Do you like to hang on to stuff – 'just in case'?

What would happen if you were to Flip It and become a purger rather than a hoarder? Terrifying? Good.

By getting rid of your old 'stuff' you free up energy, create space and access more mental bandwidth to help you think more creatively and clearly.

The challenging part of being a purger is getting started. After years of holding on to stuff 'just in case', having a major clear out can be a bit traumatic. That's why you need to change your thinking and Flip It into a challenge.

Could you fill 10 bin bags? Or even 20? What about ordering a skip! That's what Anne Holliday did when I challenged her, and she filled

it! Anne told me, 'Once I got over the mental block of throwing things away, I became obsessed with filling that skip.' Anne also gave bags full of goodies to charity shops and good causes. 'It was a goal,' said Anne, 'and I always achieve my goals.'

I know you hear stories of people who discover a priceless artefact in their attic which they nearly threw out years ago. But the reason why you hear about that is because it's so rare. If you don't need it or use it, chuck it.

So while we're on the subject of purging, how full is your wardrobe? The chances are it's packed with clothes you don't wear and never will. I have friends who go shopping and 'can't find anything' to buy. Could their sub-conscious be saying, 'Don't buy it, you've got something just like that at home', or 'Put it back, there isn't anywhere to hang it'! If that's you, then here's a simple and extremely effective way to sort out your wardrobe.

After you've worn something and it's time to put it back in your wardrobe, hang it up on the right-hand side. When a month or two has passed, go through your clothes, starting from the far left and take out two thirds. This is the pile that needs to go to the charity shop, be sold on eBay, given to friends or chucked. Don't allow it back in the wardrobe unless there is a very compelling reason why you should keep it.

Think about it. You wear 10 per cent of your clothes 90 per cent of the time. You'll never again wear some stuff and much of your wardrobe needs a major overhaul.

We were coaching a couple recently who wanted to sell some clothes and were wondering the best way to do this. After a little Flip It thinking we came up with the idea of having a social event where you could bring your unwanted clothes, try on others, swap them, buy new ones and have a fun time too. The best bit was the name: 'The Try On, The Switch in The Wardrobe!'

Flip Bit

Don't keep clothes because they 'may come back' – retro takes a minimum of 20 years. Don't keep small clothes because you're going to lose weight. Chuck them, switch them or sell them. You can have new ones as a reward when you've found your new shape.

Safer, stress-free, happier driving

Driving is consistently listed as one of the top five most stressful activities. Can you Flip It? I think so. Here are a few simple ways to turn this tiresome form of transport into a journey of joy.

- **The MPG challenge:** I used to race to my office and get frustrated when I was held up. As the traffic built up I would become more and more agitated. Not such a healthy way to drive, I'm sure you'll agree. Then I got a new car which had a miles per gallon (MPG) read out. I decided to Flip my driving style and set a new goal, 'What's the best MPG I can get on a journey?'

As my driving style changed, my blood pressure dropped, my fuel bills were reduced and I'm sure I became a safer driver.

Even if your car doesn't have a 'live' read out you can still play the game each time you fill up.

- **Super courteous:** The super courteous driver really knows how to Flip It with style. The idea is simplicity itself. Rather than getting angry with people driving too fast or too slowly, blocking you in or pulling out in front of you, simply allow and encourage them to do so (safely). Let two people out in front of you at a junction, give away a parking space. Say a big 'thank you' (to yourself) when a truck is hogging the overtaking lane on a bank. Turn it into a game, but play safe.

- **Four-wheel university:** If you spend just 1 hour a day in your car and, rather than listening to music on the radio, you choose to listen to educational, motivational and instructional CDs, in a year you will have listened to over 200 hours of material from some of the finest brains on the planet.

It's like a bonus month of full-time education with some extra night classes thrown in. Audio learning is a brilliant way to Flip It and turn often banal radio into something brilliant.

Flip It with numbers

When you Flip It and think about numbers in different ways some amazing things will happen. Here are a couple of simple little number challenges.

The next time you order food from a takeaway that has a numeric menu, I challenge you to order using your date of birth. I was born on 9 July 1967 so my order would be a number 9, a 7 and a 67. To really challenge yourself, try ordering this way without looking at the menu at all and just see what turns up!

If you'd like a change from horoscopes then Flip It and find out your 'Nine Star Ki'. This is an ancient Japanese system that uses your birth date to determine your personality type and behaviours. I'm a six and you know what they say about sixes!

Ironic Flip Bit

Have you noticed the bad design and lousy layout of most feng shui websites?

Using Flip It

I asked some of the wonderful members of my online community at www.michaelheppell.com for some examples of how they used Flip It thinking. Here are a couple of their responses.

A fertile mind

My 'horse dung principle' goes something like this.

Horse dung – to a horse it's a useless and worthless pile of waste but to a gardener it's full of nutrients and a source of growth and new life. So the next time you're faced with a pile of crap ...

Best regards

Joe Osman

Flippin' neighbours

Every Friday night I'd get a knock on the door from one of my neighbours who would call to gossip about the week they had had. It mainly covered their trials and tribulations, how depressed they were and what was wrong in the world.

One day I decided it was time to Flip this way of thinking. Just as they started to tell me about their week I broke their stride and asked them, 'How do you do that?'

'Do what?' came the reply.

'Week after week you get yourself into such a sad state. Do you wonder on the way home who you could moan to about your week? And then choose me?'

My neighbour immediately perked up and confessed nobody had ever asked them that. The best thing was they stopped in their tracks and became instantly different and immediately more likeable.

Steve Twynham

Just the job

When I was made redundant from my job three years ago I found it very worrying. I did the usual and looked at getting another job and indeed followed the traditional job-hunting track. Then it occurred to me that being made redundant was a perfect opportunity to start my own business ... in recruitment! Suddenly my redundancy became a good thing as it had been the spark that lit the desire within me to go and achieve some great things.

Regards

Adam Butler

The end bit (or the start bit if you've already Flipped It)

Thank you for buying and reading *Flip It*. What started as a phrase I used when coaching has turned into a rather splendid book (I was going to be all modest there but then decided to Flip It and be proud of my work).

Before we part I'd like to share just one more story; pay close attention as there's a test at the end.

I have a wonderful friend called Malcolm Kyle. He's one of the most positive proactive people you could ever meet. Every day he sends me an email with a story, idea or quote. A little while ago he sent me a tale which created a bit of debate around the Heppell household. Here's the story.

> There was a blind girl who hated herself because she was blind. She hated everyone, except her loving boyfriend. He was always there for her.
>
> She told her boyfriend, 'If I could only see the world, I would marry you.'
>
> One day, someone donated eyes to her. Weeks later when the bandages came off, she was able to see everything, including her boyfriend.
>
> He asked her, 'Now that you can see the world, will you marry me?' The girl looked at her boyfriend and saw that he was blind. The sight of his closed eyelids shocked her. She hadn't expected that and the thought of looking at them for the rest of her life led her to refuse his marriage proposal.
>
> Her boyfriend left with a broken heart. A few days later she received a note from him saying: 'Take good care of your eyes my dear, for before they were yours, they were mine.'

When I read the story there were a couple of gasps, then the obvious, 'It's not true. Is it?' Then the Flip It moment ... One by one everyone got it and came up with the same Flip It answer. A solution that could have fixed their dilemma years earlier. Have you worked it out yet? If so well done, you are now a fully qualified Flip It thinker!

You can celebrate now and get some goodies too, just email me your answer and as a reward I'll send you 10 bonus Flip It ideas (a couple of which were a little too wild for the book) more information can be found on the next page. And if you're still wondering, drop me an email and I'll share the Flip It answer.

End note

There are over 100 ideas for using *Flip It* and getting the best out of everything in this book and I do believe I've only scratched the surface. There are thousands of ideas and uses for Flip It which haven't made it into these pages and thousands of others which I don't know about yet – but you do. Perhaps you could share your Flip It ideas and we'll use them (with your permission) in future editions and on our website.

Our dedicated Flip It email address is flipit@michaelheppell.com for all your ideas and thoughts.

Your call to action!

Now you know how to Flip It it's time for action. Go on, test yourself. Make Flip It part of your everyday habits and behaviours. The results will be amazing, but you've got to go beyond knowing and move into doing.

The hardest part of writing a book is knowing how to finish it. Should it be dramatic? Or perhaps poignant? Maybe mysterious? I've known authors who've spent days working on their final words. Not me, you don't need a big finish when you've said everything, so I've decided to Flip It and end just like this.

Ten *free* Flip Its

You can receive 10 free additional Flip It ideas by registering for Michael Heppell's free support programme. Plus you'll get Michael Heppell's amazing *90 Days of Brilliance* online motivation and training to help you with your own personal development.

Go online to www.michaelheppell.com and simply register for *90 days of Brilliance* support programme. When you register tell us what you thought of *Flip It* and the lovely people at Michael Heppell Ltd will send you:

- 10 free additional Flip It ideas;
- a weekly *90 Days of Brilliance* programme featuring audio, video and special articles;
- a regular Michael Heppell newsletter;
- special offers for Michael Heppell live events;
- plus an opportunity to participate in live tele-seminars, access the Michael Heppell archives and be the first to hear of live events and seminars.

Contact details

Contact Michael Heppell Ltd

Tel: UK – 08456 733 336 international – +44 1434 688 555

Website: www.michaelheppell.com

Email: info@michaelheppell.com

For television and media enquiries please contact:

Michael Foster at MF Management, London

Tel: UK – 0203 291 2929 international – +44 203 291 2929

Email: mfmall@mfmanagement.com

Acknowledgements

Many authors find this a very difficult part of a book. I think spelling the word 'acknowledgements' is the toughest part! Now all I have to do is list the people who helped to make this book possible, whilst being extra careful not to miss anyone out, mix up one person with another or make it dull for you, the most important person to acknowledge, the reader! So let's start with you, the most special person in this section because without you there would be no reason to write *Flip It*. Thank you, dear reader. An author's dream is to get their book published and, an author's nightmare is that no one reads it. Thank you for reading *Flip It* and keeping the dream alive. OK, now we're off.

Next it's an easy one, my wonderful wife Christine. Here's a little secret. Christine writes my books with me, runs our business, looks after my live productions (including audio and visuals for all my events). She writes course materials, submits all the best ideas, effortlessly manages to look after all the important bits of family life and still looks as stunning now as the day we met. She does all that and I get all the credit. Christine, I'm sorry that happens. But thank you for doing it. And can we keep it just that way, please?

I'm deeply proud of my son Michael who works hard, lives our methods and is always there to help.

I am inspired by my daughter Sarah who makes me laugh so much and keeps me on my toes with my goal to be a brilliant Dad.

I'm very lucky to have Pearson, the world's greatest publishers, as my network to the world. My editor, publisher and friend, Rachael Stock, has once again pulled out all the stops for this book. Working during maternity leave is way beyond the call of duty. Thank you for having faith in *Flip It* from day one.

And a special thank you to my new editor, Elie Williams, who picked up the baton, added magic, innovation and brilliance to craft and hone *Flip It* into the book you hold today.

Thank you also to the brilliant marketing and sales teams at Pearson. Getting a book published is the easy part; ensuring every book store wants it, gets it and sells it is something else. You are the very best in the business.

The illustrations in *Flip It* are created by the amazing Steve Burke at The Design Group, Newcastle.

The photograph inside the cover was taken by Susan Bradley.

My personal team is amazing. Vanessa Thompson, Ruth Thomson, Laura Scott, Alastair Walker and Sheila Storey make everything easier, better and much more fun. Thank you for your work, creativity and patience.

We have some brilliant supporting organisations that make life much easier and pleasurable. A couple of special mentions: the Red Carnation Hotel Group provides us with our 'home away from home' in brilliant style. Datawright Computer Services and Tricycle Media supply first-class IT and web support. And Taxi Mark gets us from A to B. Thank you to you all.

It's about now where I could list hundreds of people who help to make my life better so, in the spirit of brevity, I'll simply say you know who you are. Thank you.

Additional resources and organisations mentioned in *Flip It*

Michael Heppell Ltd	www.michaelheppell.com
Pearson Education	www.pearsoned.co.uk
The Milestone Hotel	www.milestonehotel.com
Dr Fiona Ellis	www.hrwc.co.uk
Paul Mort	www.precisionfitness.co.uk
The Twelve Apostles	www.12apostleshotel.com
Richard Nugent	www.successinfootball.com
Summer Lodge	www.summerlodgehotel.co.uk
Smyth & Gibson Shirts	www.smythandgibson.com
Lifephorce	www.lifephorce.co.uk
Tim Price	www.executel.co.uk
The Design Group	www.tdgbrand.com
Malcolm Kyle	www.moso.ltd.uk